BATTERY ACTION!

BATTERY ACTION!

The Story of the 43rd (Howitzer) Battery,
Canadian Field Artillery

1916-1919

by

Hugh R. Kay, George Magee,
and Finlay MacLennan

CEF BOOKS
2002

National Library of Canada Cataloguing in Publication Data
Kay, Hugh R., 1890-1917

Battery action! : the story of the (43rd) Battery, Canadian Field Artillery, 1916-1919

Reprint. First Published: Toronto: Warwick Bros. & Rutter, 1921.
ISBN 1-896979-31-9

1. Canada. Canada Army. (Howitzer) Battery, 43rd— History. 2. World War, 1914-1918—Regimental histories—Canada. 1. Magee, George, 1891-1918. II. MacLennan, F.A. III. Title.

D547.C2K39 2002 940.4'1271 C2002-900209-5

Published by: CEF BOOKS
P.O. Box 40083
Ottawa, Ontario, Canada, K1V 0W8.
1-613-823-7000

This Publication has been supported by the Canadian War Museum.

The publisher would like to acknowledge the contributions of the Descendants and Friends of the 43rd Battery, C.F.A. Without their support and interest this book would have never been republished. The contributors are: Ken and Jean Morrison of Thunder Bay, Bruce and Jessie Glenn, Ruth Wright, Margaret Hayter, Sheila Case, John Does, J.C. Morrison, Dennis Jamieson, Mae Potton, Pamela Dickson, Geraldine Willie, Barbara June Case, Hugh and Joan Revell, Elizabeth Thompson, Cam Buchan and Helen Broadfoot. They have passed the torch.

Front cover: Detail of the painting "The Taking of Vimy Ridge, Easter Monday, 1917" by Richard Jack (1866-1952). (Canadian War Museum 8178.)

Preface to the 2002 Edition

There can be few books with a more tragic history than "Battery Action!" Both of its wartime authors died in battle. Later from their carefully-written notes which were passed on to others, the book was put together.

It started as nothing more than a few skits and stories to entertain the boys of the 43rd Howitzer Battery, Canadian Field Artillery at Christmas 1916, but grew into the personal story of those men and their times.

Hugh Kay wrote the first two parts of the book, the first at Christmas 1916 and the second in September 1917, just before the Battle of Passchendaele. Kay was a 26 year-old Scot, one of the original University of Toronto (Knox College) recruits in the Battery, and one of the great characters in the unit. He had served with the Battery since it arrived in France in July 1916 and had gained some distinction as a signaller, winning the Military Medal for bravery. The popular Kay had planned for future installments.

On November 6th, 1917 Hugh Kay, an officer and two other signallers accompanied the leading waves of infantry in the assault on Passchendaele village. The men were to act as spotters. They would relay information to the artillery batteries to support the soldiers in their attack. While advancing through heavy shelling the officer was wounded and taken out of the fighting by one of the men. Hugh Kay and the other signaller continued on. They established a position and sent back reports to the guns. During the shelling Kay was wounded, but he refused to leave his post. Later they were relieved and Signaller Kay reported to an Advanced Dressing Station to have his wound tended to. While awaiting treatment Hugh Reid Kay was killed instantly by the explosion of a German shell. He was a great loss to the Battery.

His comrades were not deterred by his death. Hugh's old manuscript was retrieved from his personal belongings, and his tradition of recording the life and times of the 43rd (Howitzer) Battery, Canadian Field Artillery was passed to George Magee.

William George Magee was also an original member of the 43rd, and in the spirit of Hugh Kay, wrote what became Part II of the Battery's

story. At Christmas 1917, Magee entertained the men with his installment of humorous events and anecdotes. Over the spring and summer of 1918 Magee did not add to his story. Perhaps out of a healthy respect for Kay's fate, he avoided penning any other episodes. But the curse seemed to run undeterred, and after George Magee had been safely at war for more than two years, surviving the Battles of the Somme, Vimy, Passchendaele, Amiens, and Arras, his time ran out.

With a little more than a month remaining in the war, in one of the final battles, 100,000 men of the Canadian Corps attacked across the Canal du Nord and smashed the German defenses in front of Cambrai. But casualties amongst the Canadians were heavy and amongst the wounded was George Magee. George was quickly evacuated to a Casualty Clearing Station just south of Arras, but his wounds were severe. On September 28th, 1918 George Magee died. He was 27.

The war was now almost over. The men of the 43rd Battery, CFA were safely out of danger and their time together at an end. But during those years 1916-1919 they had become an intensely devoted group. Their loyalty and respect for one another were formed in a caldron of emotion few who have not experienced war could comprehend. Driven by that devotion the survivors chose to finish the job started by their fallen comrades. This task fell to Finlay MacLennan, Ben Case and Andrew Lane.

Even in 1919 the men were aware of passing on their legacy, a testament to their times and sacrifices, and with that uppermost in their minds they put together Part III of "Battery Action!" Both MacLennan and Lane were University of Toronto (Knox College) boys and original members of the Battery. Andrew Lane had been wounded twice; once on the Somme in 1916 and again at Passchendaele in 1917. MacLennan spent more than two years with the 43rd at the Front. Benson Case, also from Knox College, served in the 5th Field Ambulance from September 1915 until he transferred to the 43rd Battery in July 1916. Like the others he spent his entire war with the Battery. The three used what had been salvaged of Magee's and Kay's notes and talked and wrote to many ex-members of the Battery. In 1920 the book was finally published and the legacy preserved.

In spite of its origins "Battery Action!" is far from sad. It is about the men of the 43rd Battery, 1916-1919, and serves as a testament to their courage, humour and optimism. It is a monument to the memory of great days. There is no indication that the authors were working with the shadow of death hanging over them. Theirs is a buoyant and happy story that looks for a joke in every situation and records their daily life in the style of a diary. "Battery Action!" is a very human document with many little touches that all can appreciate. It gives an exceptional view into the life of an artilleryman in the Great War and is a unique contribution to the literature of the period.

As an added touch the book uses the sketches of an unknown cartoonist by the name of Jimmie Frise. Frise, who had served as a driver in the 12th Battery, CFA, would later become well-known from his many collaborations with Canadian storyteller, Gregory Clark (also a First World War vet).

But the publishing of "Battery Action!" in 1920 was not the end of the story of the 43rd Battery, CFA. The closeness of the men was kept alive through the Forty Third Battery Association. The Association issued a newsletter, called The Battery Bulletin, on a regular basis (in 1974 they had produced 92 issues). The Battery Bulletin kept members up-to-date with their old comrades. Although in the later issues the "In Memoriam" column and "The Sick List" grew longer, it always maintained that cheerfulness so typical of the men themselves.

Then there were the never-to-be-missed Annual Reunions held each October in Toronto. There the old soldiers would enjoy Canal du Nord Sole with Vimy Sauce, Shrap peas, Muster Rolls, followed by Whiz Bang Puffs and Perky Coffee. The dinner ceremony would always include a Silent Toast and Messages from Absentees, and conclude with Auld Lang Syne and Stand Down.

By 1981 the Old Comrades were on their 63rd Reunion! Even in the face of their dwindling ranks a sense of humour held on. The final six survivors were to share a bottle of scotch. (The story goes that they did not wait until only six remained, and that the scotch was unpalatable.)

Today no one remains of the 43rd (Howitzer) Battery, Canadian Field Artillery. Time has finally claimed the lives that the Germans could not.

But the strength of their loyalty and their unflagging commitment to their times live on. They have been passed from one generation to another.

It is with a sincere respect that "Battery Action!" is once again returned to the present and is dedicated to, as the old 43rd vet Bill Swain said in 1974, ". . . the old boys whom I knew in days gone by, a long, long time ago."

Norm Christie
Ottawa, Ontario
March, 2002

Some Notes on Organization and Artillery

When war was declared in August 1914 Canada had a permanent Army of only 3,000 men. This included infantry, engineers, cavalry, medical units and artillery. None-the-less the Canadian Government offered to raise a force of 25,000 men. This was accomplished by thousands of men, many serving in Canadian Militia Regiments, coming forward to volunteer. The First Contingent of 30,000 men was sent overseas in October 1914. A Second Contingent sailed in the Summer of 1915, and the Third Contingent, which included the 43rd Battery, later in the year.

The 43rd Battery was like most other units raised in the war. It drew enthusiastic men from the militia (the Reserves), like the Knox College boys, and volunteers from all walks of life. This always led to an unusual mix of characters. The units were usually commanded by important businessmen, politicians and the like from the local community. The CO of the 43rd was Colonel McCrae, an important man in Guelph.

However the surge to enlist resulted in Canada raising so many units that most would never see action. In fact more than 100 Artillery Batteries were raised in Canada during the war. Each battery was allotted a block of Service Numbers distinct to the Battery. The block given to the 43rd was 307601 to 308600. The originals had Service Numbers starting with 307, consequently in the book the originals are often referred to as 307s.

Most of the Batteries would be shipped to England and there be broken up to provide reinforcements to the artillery batteries serving with the Canadian Corps at the Front. The 43rd Battery was fortunate enough to serve as a battery on active service from July 1916 until the end of the war.

It was at first a Battery in the 10th Brigade, CFA, a member of the Third Canadian Infantry Division. It remained with the Third through the Battle of the Somme and the Capture of Vimy Ridge. In the summer of 1917 the artillery was once again reorganized and the 43rd became part of the 8th Army Brigade, CFA, under the command of the Canadian Corps. They fought at Hill 70, Passchendaele, in the German Offensives of March-April 1918, the Advance to Victory, which included the great Battles of Amiens, Arras, the Canal du Nord and Cambrai. They were at Jemappes, near Mons in the last days of the war.

I have added a few explanatory notes to help understand the responsibilities of a Field Artillery Battery during the Great War.

Organization

The British forces (British Expeditionary Force) on the Western Front, which included the Canadians, were divided into five Armies. Each army, consisting of a number of Army Corps, could contain more than 500,000 men. The Army was an Administrative, logistical and planning operation. Battle units, such as infantry and artillery, were part of the Army Corps. Through most of the war the Canadians were a part of the First British Army. An Army was commanded by a General and the BEF was commanded by a Field Marshall.

An Army Corps consisted of a varying number of Infantry Divisions, depending on its needs, and often contained more than 100,000 men. For most of the war all four Canadian Divisions (20,000 men each) made up the Canadian Corps. In addition to the Divisions, the Corps also was directly responsible for heavy garrison (and some field or mobile) artillery, cavalry, cyclists, labour battalions, etc., known as Corps Troops. These resources would be allocated to assist the Infantry Divisions as required. (During a reorganization of the artillery in 1917 the 43rd Howitzer Battery transferred to the 8th Army Brigade, CFA. becoming Corps Troops.) An Army Corps was commanded by a Lieutenant-General.

The Infantry Division consisted of 20,000 men, including 12,000 infantry and 3,500 artillerymen. The Division was broken down into three Infantry Brigades. Each Brigade had four infantry battalions (4,000 men) and a brigade of Field Artillery (to provide support for the infantry). The Artillery Brigade consisted of four batteries of field artillery (this varied in the earlier stages of the war). Three of the batteries were made up of six 18 pounder guns, while the fourth was always a six gun Howitzer battery. (The 43rd was originally a four gun Howitzer battery, reorganized into a six gun battery, and sent to France in July 1916 with the 10th CFA Brigade, supporting the Third Canadian Infantry Division. It remained with the Third Division until July 1917, when it became Corps Troops, as part of the 8th Army Brigade, CFA.)

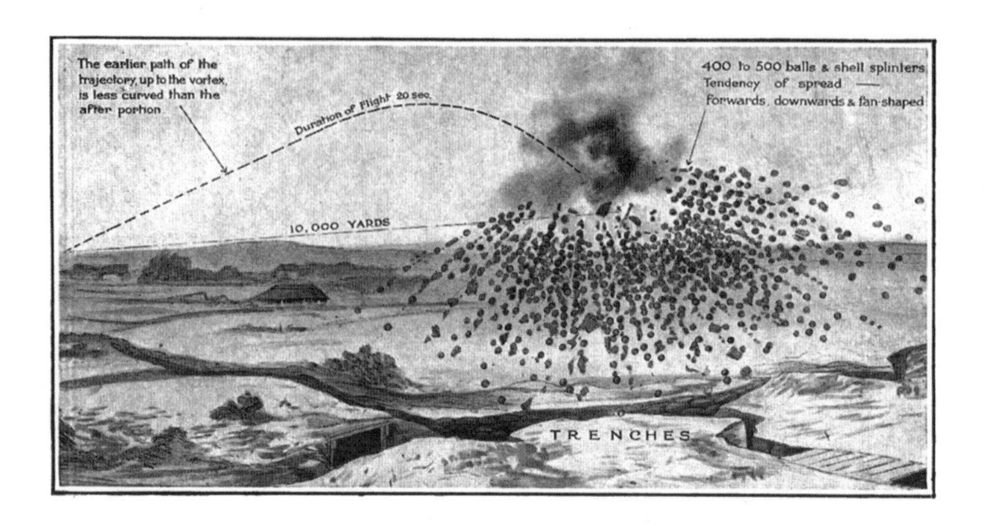

The Power Of The Field Artillery Shells.
Shrapnel shell breaking over enemy communication trenches and scattering 400 balls.

The Power Of The Field Artillery Shells.
High-Explosive shell breaking fortified enemy entrenchments.

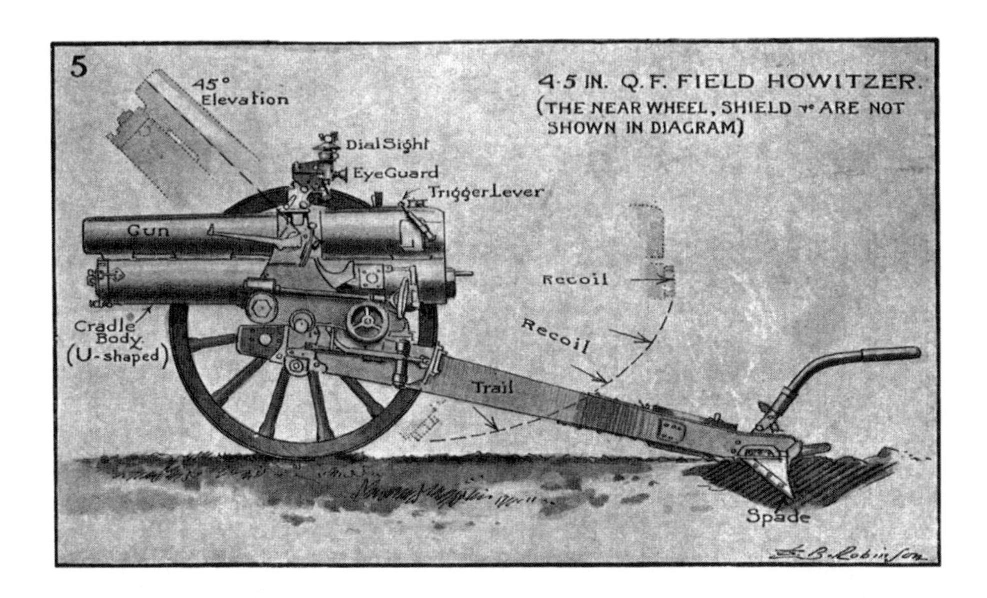

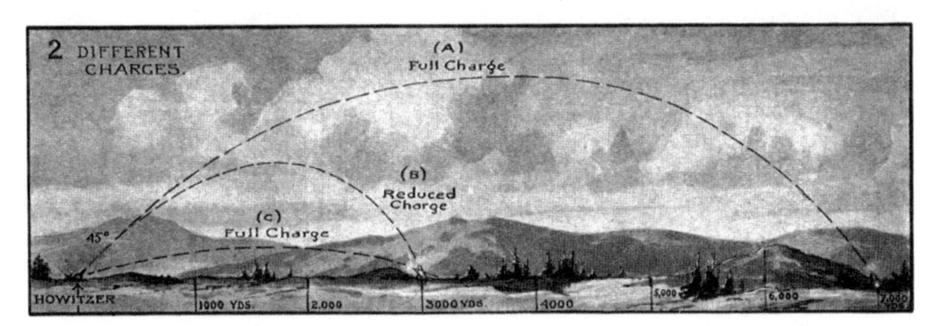

(A) Represents a howitzer firing a full charge with 45 deg. elevation to 7,000 yards' range.

(B) Shows the trajectory at 3,000 yards with a reduced charge.

(C) Shows a hit at 3,000 yards, with the full charge and reduced elevation.

The Field Artillery Battery

There were two basic types of field artillery batteries; those that contained 18 pounder guns and those firing 4.5" Quick-Firing (QF) Howitzers. The 43rd was a Howitzer battery. In 1916 a Howitzer Battery consisted of four guns and 137 men, including gunners, bombardiers, signallers, drivers, fitters, shoesmiths, cooks, wheelers, saddlers, grooms and farriers. By 1918 a Howitzer Battery of six guns consisted of 196 men and 169 horses or mules.

The men of the battery were responsible for all facets of the artillery operation, including maintenance of equipment and wagons, grooming and feeding the horses or mules, supplying shells to the front, etc.

The 4.5" QF Howitzer

The artillery piece used by the 43rd Battery was the 4.5 Quick-Firing Howitzer. It fired a 4.5" diameter shell that weighed 35 lbs. The shell could fire either High Explosive or Shrapnel shells within a range of 7,200 yards. Its muzzle velocity was 1,010 feet per second. What differentiates the howitzer from the 18 pounders was the muzzle velocities and the maximum elevation of the gun barrel. The 18 pounder was designed to elevate to 16%, whereas the howitzer could raise its barrel to 45%. The curved trajectory of the howitzer allowed it to hit targets that were concealed or placed behind natural obstructions such as dugouts, enemy material dumps, communication trenches and opposing artillery emplacements. Shrapnel shells were used to cut barbed wire and against infantry. High Explosive (HE) shells were used against protected targets.

The Canadian Artillery, 1914-1918

Throughout the Great War Canada's artillery performed exceptionally well. Their efficiency was a major factor in the victory at Vimy Ridge. At Hill 70 they smashed countless German counter-attacks with deadly accuracy. Their courage and tenacity against deplorable conditions and German HE and gas saved the day at Passchendaele. Their contribution to the success of the Canadian Corps should not be forgotten.

Although most artillerymen were not often in the front line, they were never far away. Death could arrive at any moment in the form of

German HE or shrapnel, or even worse, gas shells. In addition the guns themselves could be lethal due to a worn barrel or a defective shell. During the First World War 44,000 men served in the Canadian Artillery. Their battle casualties amounted to 10,097, including 2,565 dead.

The Interior of a Shrapnel shell.

A is the charge of powder which forces the bullets from the casing; B the charge, exploded by the firing device E, which expels the shell from the gun. The copper driving band is seen at C; and D is the fuse head with timing apparatus.

Introduction to the 2002 Edition

The 43rd Battery, CFA (Canadian Field Artillery) was a most interesting, and somewhat unusual outfit. The fact that it was recruited by Colonel David McCrae, father of John McCrae of "In Flanders Fields" fame is one source of distinction. The McCraes were a military family of long standing in the Guelph area, and at the age of 70 when most would consider themselves retired, McCrae senior raised the 43rd Battery and took it overseas, although he himself was not permitted to take it into action.

In addition to being prominent soldiers the McCraes were pillars of the Presbyterian Church, and McCrae himself a temperance advocate. This connection doubtless assisted in convincing a goodly number the theological students of the Presbyterian seminary, Knox College in the University of Toronto, to journey to Guelph and join the McCrae battery. Whether the fair Miss Cockburn, mentioned early in the book, was directly the colonel's agent, or just accidentally filled that role, cannot be determined at this time. This core of Knox students, plus Colonel McCrae's Presbyterian credentials, caused the battery for a time to be dubbed "The Presbyterian Battery". There were other influences too. Since many in the battery were university students, the battery contained many young men who were potential officers, although there is no indication that great numbers seized this opportunity. The future temperance crusader and moderator of the United Church of Canada, listed in the book as a Sergeant J.R. Mutchmor, did receive a commission, although it may have been in the chaplaincy corps. A number of comments in the book indicate that battery members did not hold the role of officer in very high regard with demands in war time for peace time spit and polish being particularly resented.

However Colonel McCrae, and a few others were sincerely admired. Former officers played little role in the post-war 43rd Battery Association which was dominated by men who had served as non-commissioned officers. Since the battery contained a very educated group of men destined for a calling which would see them stand up in front of large audiences and "perform" it is hardly surprising that an undergraduate type self-entertainment based on the foibles of individuals everyone knew and common experiences should appear to create moments of cheer in the middle of the grim and grinding tasks of war. The scripts of these frontline self-entertainments lovingly preserved in battered kit bags form the core of the material in this book. As will be seen, the first two scriptwriters, both of whom were killed in action, were the especially talented in this area, with later writers lacking quite their light touch, being a bit more cynical, and also probably conscious that the material they had on hand would make a fine informal battery history.

Within this context something should be said about the general achievements of the Canadian artillery in the First World War under the direction of Brigadier General Andy McNaughton, later to be well known as the commander of the Canadian 1st Corps early in World War II. During the early years of the World War 1 counter battery work consisted of lobbing hundreds of shells in the general direction of a target on the assumption that by reasonable odds some of these shells would hit their objective. Needless to say this was very expensive of ammunition and the shell shortage of the middle years of the war caused some of the bolder minds in the British Empire's artillery to seek ways of making this operation more efficient and effective. The leading Canadian in this regard was McNaughton. He experimented with improved gun flash spotting and sound locating to the point where when an enemy gun fired his staff could quickly and very accurately map its location. Aerial spotting from planes and balloons assisted the process. Greater efficiency in destroying the enemy's guns was achieved by taking into account such factors as gun wear, wind direction, temperature, and barometric pressure. At its most successful late in the war McNaughton's guns with two shells could knock out an enemy battery where previously required the expenditure of one hundred. The Canadian counter battery work came to be without peer both on the Allied and enemy side.

The 43rd, with its well-educated rank-and-file, was a natural to handle the sophisticated gadgetry needed to bring McNaughton's ideas to a successful reality. It is interesting that tactical bombers of the Royal Air Force in the Second World War went through a similar evolution towards accuracy as the war progressed.

In addition to the dedications in the original book, we would like to add a dedication to the memory of Ben S. Case, one of the editors of this book, mentioned therein from time to time as Old Ben. Since Ben was at best just a couple of years older than the ordinary 43rd Battery gunner one has to assume that this nickname came from the fact that Ben was, when the battery first saw action, an old soldier having joined the unit in Flanders after serving for a time with the 5th Field

Ambulance. Ben not only had a hand in this book's production, but he was a key figure in the maintenance of the Forty Third Battery Association as its long-time secretary and newsletter editor. During the Thirties he and some buddies from the battery bought a farm just west of Georgetown, Ontario, dividing it into four with Ben taking the old farm house, using it as a weekend retreat, and eventually retiring there. Ben was the host of annual battery picnics in June for many years (and 5th Field Ambulance picnics also). The picnics ended only when Ben at the age of 90 was forced to give up "Dead Horse Farm" and enter a senior citizens home. To a host of the children and grandchildren of battery and ambulance veterans Ben Case was Uncle Ben, as he was to my wife, her siblings and cousins. A bachelor, Ben had an infinite capacity for friendship. His generosity and friendship both to his veteran friends and to his adopted Esquesing township were a blessing to all who knew him. He was the type of person whose self-effacing good works may not bring him the Order of Canada, but who deserves to be honoured none the less.

Ken Morrison,
Thunder Bay, Ontario.

Preface to the 1920 Edition

While we realize that introductory remarks are a conventional evil -which, fortunately, is serenely ignored by most readers - still, a few words of explanation appear necessary in connection with the publication of this volume. It has not been an individual enterprise but solely in response to the wide-spread demand of former members of the battery that the history of the 43rd, which Hugh Kay and George Magee recorded for our amusement during the war till their task was cut short by death, should be completed and published, in a more permanent form.

Almost four years have passed by since the night of Christmas, 1916, when to the laughing audience assembled in an Aubigny estaminet Hugh Kay read his amusing chronicles. Written hastily, on short notice, simply to pass a social hour and with no idea of publication, his sketch is so faithful a portraiture of well-known battery figures that with ever-increasing interest we read the dialogues and personal glimpses in its pages and each line calls up old memories, more poignant because not only Kay but so many of whom he wrote have passed out to that haven where "the weary are at rest."

We can add nothing to the tribute which George Magee has paid to Kay in the opening paragraphs of his continuation of the history of the battery. Peculiarly appropriate in his case seems; the description which has been handed down to us of the famous Chevalier Bayard - "sans peur et sans reproche." After seventeen months' continuous and hazardous service, in which he had earned the respect and admiration of all, he was killed the morning the Canadians took Passchendaele, November 6th, 1917, while engaged up forward in a dangerous task for which he had volunteered.

When, a little later, Christmas found the battery out on rest in Ohlain, George Magee read to us additional chapters, which Kay had found time to write during the summer, and then, with considerable reluctance, his own annals. No mistake had been made in choosing George Magee as Kay's successor in the role of historian, for he was not only blessed with a sense of humor but a retentive memory which stored up a fund of ludicrous situations or utterances. Upon first meeting him, one received the impression of a strong man, not only in physique but in heart and mind. Often silent to the point of taciturnity, with a reserve only penetrated upon longer acquaintance, he more

THE LATE HUGH R. KAY, M.M.

Who was killed in action at Passchendale, Nov. 6th, 1917.

(From a last letter to his father.)

"I have been in some close corners, yet my temperament has remained surprisingly buoyant all through, possibly because of a rather childlike trust in th Great Disposer of all things, to which I freely testify, and to a mind of varied interests, which has kept me from brooding in too morbid a way on the tragic side of this war. Then last, but not least, because of a willingness to die, if need be, in this cause."

THE LATE GEORGE MAGEE

Who died of wounds received in action near Bourlon Wood, Sept. 26th, 1918.

"He scarce had need to doff his pride or
slough the dross of earth—
E'en as he trod that day to God so
walked he from his birth,
In simpleness and gentleness and honour
and clean mirth.

So cup to lip in fellowship they gave him
welcome high
And made him place at the banquet
board—the Strong Men ranged
thereby,
Who had done his work and held his
peace and had no fear to die."

often kept in the background when a number were talking and jesting, but, while he took little part in the conversation, none of it escaped him. Usually a well-filled pipe was between his teeth and an inimitable smile half playing upon his lips, an odd smile, peculiarly his own, which he seemed to try to suppress.

There was not a harder-working man in the battery, nor one less sparing of himself despite frequent periods of ill-health. As brave as he was silent, as considerate as he was strong - a man's man was George Magee. It was inevitable that his modest avoidance of the limelight and reserved manner should preclude recognition of his sterling merits in an army where, too often, the path of promotion lay through petty ostentation and servility. But George Magee won that which is infinitely more precious, which abides after decorations, stripes and "pips" have been discarded - the lasting and reverent remembrance of all who came in contact with him.

Like his predecessor, Magee did not live to complete the story of the battery but fell by his gun just after the 43rd galloped into action across the Canal du Nord, September 27th, 1918. We were fortunate in securing his manuscript for inclusion here and one felt compelled to handle reverently those water-stained pages, brown from a year's travel in haversack or blanket-roll at the front, with his clear handwriting in indelible lead like a voice from the past.

Where all have so generously assisted us in concluding the battery history - some by furnishing material, some by friendly criticism, others by lending diaries and snapshot albums, and all by encouraging interest - it were invidious to mention names. To all we owe grateful thanks and we hope that this book, towards the publication of which nearly all the old boys of the battery have contributed in some shape or form, will not prove entirely disappointing but recall old scenes and associations which are fast becoming dimmer and vaguer in our memories.

F. A. MacLennan,
Ben Case,
Andrew Lane,
Editors.

TO THE SACRED MEMORY
OF THOSE BRAVE MEN WHO FELL IN ACTION
WITH THE 43RD BATTERY, C.F.A.,
DURING THE GREAT WAR,
THIS BOOK IS RESPECTFULLY
DEDICATED.

Table of Contents

S.R.D.
FRISE

PART I

Chapter I - 1

Aubigny, Christmas 1916

I suppose that, like all other Scotchmen in this Battery, I should have an "interrupter" (I mean interpreter) before trying to speak to you, but I will make every effort to be plain, and it is quite likely that before I have finished you will understand all too, plainly what I mean.

When I was first asked by Mr. Youell to make up a history of the movements and doings of this Battery during the past eleven months, I thought of the following story. The speaker is a Tommy who is waiting to, go over the top with his platoon. He remarks to his sergeant "I suppose in a few moments Sarge, we shall be making 'istory." "'istory, be blowed," replied the sergeant "what you have to make is geography." So I said at first with the sergeant, "'istory, be blowed", but Mr. Youell insisted. "Go as far as you like Kay", he said, sort of careless like; so I carried on and went as far as I liked and perhaps further than some of you would like.

But the more I thought of the movements of this Battery, the more I saw what a heavy job it was. Then I said to myself with James Niven McFaul, one-time theological student, "That's the worst of it," and wondered if I was in any sense fit for the job but, being one who likes to try most things at least once, I felt willing to try even this, even if it did mean a lot of work. It meant writing in cloudy corners of noisy estaminets, or in windy corners of harness rooms, or propped up in the blankets at night with everyone cursing the candle - together with G.S. Wilson. So you will judge the result in the light of these conditions. If there are any disagreeable, personal remarks made which 'get your goat' or 'untether your nanny,' or 'abduct your chamois', be sure that they are all intentional, for in a war such as this, we all shoot to kill and we are all out for blood. In any case, preparing this got me out of doing anything for a day or two and that is always worth something.

The first news I ever heard of this Battery was from a lady friend called Miss "Clara" Cockburn, who has the prettiest dark eyes (the kind with the long dark lashes) and the neatest trimmest waistline you ever saw. In our set we discuss questions of the day, such as, "Was the King mounted or dis-

mounted?" Another is - Miss Cockburn, does she or does she not wear corsets? But even if she does wear corsets - and most of us have decided that she does -"Clara" has no end of nerve. You have got to hand it to her on that score. She personally conducted a bunch of young preachers, who were anxious to fight from their comfortable nest in St. George Street, Toronto, to the Armouries in Guelph, and allowed them to run around loose with the rough men there who drank their whisky neat and smoked and chewed all the time.

However, Glory be! the Knox College angels have fallen from grace and show signs of making good soldiers. When we look at such a shining example as "Tubby" Turnbull, we have to admit that "he's good." He is responsible for coining some of the wittiest remarks about certain of the officers, N.C.O's and men of this Battery. Unfortunately, they are unprintable. Then Sergeant Mutchmor has turned out well, but as Big Nigger Jim Moss says, "An awful feller to argur, even when he knows he's wrong", adds Jim.

Guelph Days

Well! the Guelph days were short, and now they are half-forgotten. About all most of us remember is the sore heels we used to have as a result of route-marching in the Army boots, which chafed our tender feet; the "physical torture" or physical jerks or whatever you like to call it, the appetite we worked up for meals and the numberless times we marched up the street to the familiar tune of Left! Left! Left! right Left! One two Three four Left! There was Bombardier Buss, an aspiring Sergeant, with his "Cut out the talkin' there" (not a word being said), "Steady in the ranks there" (not a movement visible). We soon learned that Ex-Lieutenant Corp. Hill's middle name was "Double." Bombardier Pettitt was very much affected by our aches and pains and more merciful than most of the others. Sergeant Neelands was never very keen on "physical torture" himself - mal-de-tete, possibly, and dark brown taste in the mouth.

Well, we did learn that Colonel McCrae was a God-fearing gentleman who hated "booze" and saw that every man took the oath properly; that we were "a fine looking body of men"; and that we were a far better battery than the 29th. They being a bunch of half-soused rough-necks, while we were the "model battery" the "Presbyterian battery", the "dry battery", the "buttermilk brigade", and so forth. It was about this time that we were let in on the fact that "'tion" meant "A-Hun" to Mr. Youell and "A-Hen" to Mr. Crowe, "'tion" (childish voice) to Mr. Cockburn, while Sergeant-Major Purvis, who flashed fire from his eyes and never missed a chance of reminding us that he "had a rank", mystified the whole battery for a few weeks with his rapid-fire of "Poof! Down!, Poof! Down!, Poof! Down!" We could all say with Lautenslayer, "I didn't know for a while what in H— he was trying to get through him."

When will we ever forget Corporal White,(then in charge of the famous "C"sub) with his "All correct, Sergeant-Major," or "all sick, one absent, sir," or better still, "Fours about should put you right". In those days Bombardier Fletcher was "the ideal soldier", and the way be used to manouevre those men around in the "box-stall" at the end of the winter fair building was a sight; while Bob Reade's fine Scotch bur-r-r could be heard high above the confused din of yelling which went on during drill hours.

Do you remember how the whole Battery used to be out of step with Stevenson, and how hard it was for them to get back into step with him? Even the Sergeant-Major's copious profanity made no impression on Stevenson - or on the battery.

Then you remember how Bill Thompson used to all but assault the officers, turn about, so that he might get a place in the overseas draft; and when they turned to others and left him unsatisfied, how he would stagger off, muttering about the birth, upbringing and general character of the officers, including the O.C. Then he would walk up the main street of Guelph, , steering a course which can best be described as "beaucoup zig-zag."

Every day Buglers Dobson and Williams stumbled through something that sounded like "Fall-In" and then Bob Purvis, his eyes flashing fire and in staccato tones, abused the battery for five minutes. We tramped the roads to the tune of "One keg of beer amongst the four of us" or "She said she had a sweetheart who was going far away" that or doubled around the winter fair building with great coats on.

In the meantime Q.M.S. Ball had fitted every man with some sort of clothes, giving special attention to those whom he called "Black Presbyterians". Billy Patton spent his time worrying the aforesaid because none of the clothes issued to him would fit, for Billy was still dreaming of tailor-made clothes. Gunner Ballantyne was getting his pants "pegged" at the local tailors. Having but one pair of these, our ruddy-faced friend was forced to wait in undress uniform while the tailor did his work. In these days Gunner Ballantyne is said to have shaved morning and evening, used cold cream quite freely, and to have gone to an average of two social gatherings each and every evening with an after-church session on Sunday.

To say that the Guelph people were kind is to put it mildly but finally the night came when we stood loaded to the guards in the crowded winter-fair building for the last time. There were rivers of people on the streets which flowed back to form a regular avenue of humanity, down which we struggled to the waiting train.

Afterwards some of us remembered the rather pathetic picture which Hector Cowan presented after he had been embraced by all his relatives. Gunner Ballantyne too had to take leave of all his lady friends. They crowded around the open window of one car to be finally raised up to his level, where he kissed them all, individually, collectively, and every other way. When he had finished them all, the "Missanabie Special" pulled out, Greenlee being on guard in the corridor under protest, and Billy Patton on guard over Reggie Neelands - it was necessary for Billy to stay on guard for several days.

"They're off!" said the Guelph people, and went home to raise a new battery.

The Trip

Perhaps, like some to whom I have spoken, you would like to forget some of the unsavoury details of the journey from Guelph to England, but let me remind you of a few facts and a few places, as there is a good deal of geography in this history. You will perhaps remember the conversation in the train the first night aboard, led by such worthies as "Scotty" Walker "Rossie", John Fox and others, which was such a revelation to some of us in the way of language; how the sides of that old troop-train were spattered with porridge next morning, and the road-bed strewn with "hot dogs". There were the route-marches at Trenton, Rivière-du-loup, and at Campbellton; then let us not forget the very simple schemes devised by some men for getting fire-water at each stopping-place, and the way in which Billy Patton's prisoner pleaded to be allowed to go; and, then the arrival at St John, N.B., in a down-pour of rain, and the marching through the city and around the wonderful harbour, to be introduced to the Missanabie.

Every man has his own story to tell about the Missanabie. C.W. and P.C.Curzon and Ashley Shonk will have a very empty story, as they both faithfully fed the fishes with the few meals which they had. Both of them are quite certain that everything came up including the moon. There is the story of those who never missed a meal; the story of those who slept down by the propellers and that story will be a sort of nightmare. However, the men down there were cheerful enough to "kid" the Reverend James Niven McFaul into believing that the submarines were going to sink the old tub every night There is the story of those who remember nothing but the smell in that dining-room and the stuff called "Liver-and-Tripe" which caused a near-riot and gave rise to that expressive couplet -

"They want us to work, and they want us to fight:
How the hell can we do it on liver and tripe"

Some did all-night guards on the wind-swept deck while others did it in the officers' quarters, and testified to riotous doings there at times. The report got around, too, that Lieutenant "Clara" Cockburn played poker steadily day after day. Doug Crowe was clearly "a very sick woman".

You recall the port and starboard and masthead lights of the sister ship, the Scandinavian, gleaming astern at night, which John D. Doherty was always willing to explain to the uninitiated, he having been a seaman of sorts on the Upper Lakes in his youth. There were the plunging grey cruisers which were always on the watch, the six swift destroyers, and, finally, the lights of Plymouth on March 13th.

A happy morning, that on which we left the old Missanabie there at anchor and, after steaming up Plymouth Sound in the "tenders", landed in the land of tenement houses, chimney-pots, and compartment carriages. Then followed a trip through beautiful England, which ended in a weary tramp through the mud and rain and heat and darkness from Liphook Station to Bramshott Camp. As we stumbled on through the mud we felt that the whole business was a huge mistake; that we really should never have enlisted and that we were disappointed in England.

But England looked more attractive next morning when we wakened to the bright sunshine and the sound of bagpipes. I suppose that, even if most of the men of this Battery are Canadians by birth and once despised England

and all Englishmen, by this time they have learned to take a much greater interest in England and in things English than they ever thought would be possible. At one time you judged England by the "hired man" who worked around the farms in rural Ontario, or by the "remittance man" who was a nuisance; now you judge England in terms of London or by parts of beautiful rural England which you have seen.

Bramshott Camp

We found Bramshott Camp to be well-concealed in mud as the following spasm of parody will show,

"Sure a little drop of water fell from out of the sky one day
And it nestled in a certain spot which was full of mud and clay
And when the War Office found it, it looked so damp and fair
They said suppose we grab it and put a camp right there,
So they filled it with Canadians just to make the mud piles grow
It's the only place you'll find them no matter where you go
Then they sprinkled it with rain drops just to make it nice and damp
And when they had it finished, sure they called it Bramshott Camp."

It was at Bramshott that Jack Porteous secured the position of "riding instructor". The men in the Battery were divided into the sheep, and the goats, or the "fatigue artists" and those who "followed the ponies."In addition to these we had the wig-waggers or headquarters party. Charlie Flesh became supreme in the - kitchen. Every morning it was "For gun drill tell off," or "With drag-ropes, prepare to advance." The aiming post was the flagstaff on the Y.M.C.A. Hut or the last telegraph pole on the road or the water tower. G.S. Wilson was found to be more or less of a rough rider and gave up telephony and signalling as a bad job in order that he might specialize in breaking horses. Howard, Mackenzie and Cowan, the Sarnia contingent, saw themselves riding into action under heavy fire and decided to become drivers.

In intervals of parading we all looked at England with curious eyes and did as much "soldiering" as possible. Jack Porteous must remember the night he sat on the top of "Tex" Snider in a certain ditch between Grayshott and Bramshott. Hazlemere was the most popular resort and it was generally remarked that many of the English girls were a rather free and easy lot.

We got first leave in Bramshott, and most of us went to London to see the sights. Now almost every man discovered that he had friends in London, and lots of them, if he cared to own them. In future years the siren smiles of the women who are woefully wise will live in our memories. But most of us found London a great revelation and will never forget it. It was the largest, the best, the wickedest, the most beautiful and the ugliest city that many of us had ever seen or ever will see.

Most important of all at Bramshott, the command of the Battery passed into the hands of Captain W.A. Irving and Colonel McCrae left us, taking with him the respect and esteem of every man, without exception, in the unit.

Witley Camp

Then in April we were off to Witley with balky horses stalling all the way and an immense amount of sweat lost. Porteous tried conclusions with a plate glass window and got away with it unhurt. (I mean that he got away with it not that he got away with the window). Gunning took a header into the Devil's Punch Bowl and he too got away with it. The drivers found that certain new and strange oaths came naturally to them and they knew that this was what they had been wanting to say all along.

At Witley Camp, Captain (now Major) Irving commenced going after the Battery without gloves. You will remember the gun drill in the park with the dust drifting across in clouds, the only change being that now the aiming point shifted from the tower of Charterhouse School to the left chimney of the red cottage in the hollow. Those were long days on Hankley Common and, with all due respect to one who "went west" in the performance of his duty, let us recall the many times the battery was drawn up at close interval and a soft English voice said, "There ah a few points I wish to speak about. The driving in the last movement was very pooah. You must get the teams away moah quickly. etc. Ah there any questions you wish to ask?"(And Sergeant Mutchmor would oblige.) "We will now take up an open position, myself dismounted in front, my directah man, Neelands, dismounted 50 yahds in the reah. Mt Youell, you will bring in the battery as quickly as possible. Trumpetah!" Then, with a thunder of hooves, the black charger would be off over the common.

Sergeant-Major Purvis made himself immortal in Witley with his machine-gun delivery on parade, and his historic addresses to the battery. For example it is morning parade, and the Sergeant-Major's delivery is a little swifter than usual, "Flanks of fours, poof! down! poof! down! poof! down!". Voice from an adjoining hut takes up the refrain, "Woof! woof! woof! woof!". Acting-Orderly-Sergeant Shonk puts his head inside the door of the hut and says mildly, "Don't laugh at our Sergeant-Major."

"Steady in the ranks there! Blank Blankety Blank, Conroy, can't you stand steady for five minutes? Can't youse men understand good English? Do youse men think this is a Sunday-school picnic?" (Eyes flashing fire.) And, finally, one Sunday morning, in a burst of irreverence, "J— C—, don't you men know this is Church Parade?"

“Old Familiar Faces” Witley Camp June, 1916.

About that trip to Larkhill, perhaps the less said the better, but it at least let us see a lot of England, and get lots of fresh air. It looked like Active Service conditions; and you remember how the "dry" battery took to sleeping in breweries and on concrete floors or anywhere. Most of the time the roadside looked inviting enough. Some "covererings" (Cpl. Kay for example) went to sleep and wakened up in the arms of their section commanders. The gunners pulled the lanyard over a live shell for the first time, and saw the white smoke-bursts of time-shrapnel away across the waste lands. It was impressive to see the whole division on parade and each battery dashing into action. Sergeant Bob Reade pulled the worst boner when he lost his gun and had to pick it up with all the spare Generals looking on - but we came through, they said, with flying colours.

At Witley, Captain Donald and Lieutenant E.P. Black joined the battery or in other words "Tab" and "Edgar Pip". When old "Tab" smiled, his eyebrow slid up over his left ear and everyone around smiled. Then he took out a roan horse one day that was a sort of outlaw and rode the brute until it submitted. This gave him a reputation as a horseman, so that he won every man's respect.

The morning "Edgar Pip" arrived and appeared at morning stables, the whole Battery was sorry for him as he stood there all alone, leaning against the water-trough. For an officer he looked so lonesome that the men felt contented for once, thinking of the many friends to chum around with; and borrow money or bum cigarettes from. Many of us have since learned that, when it comes to a show-down, and there is a difficult piece of work to be done, "Edgar Pip" asks no one to go where he does not go himself. On a certain dark night he and the writer stood at the end of a hedge which bordered on an open exposed stretch. A couple of bullets went zipping past so close that you could hardly tell the difference and we both drew back. But Edgar was the first to go out and he need not have either.

It was in Witley days that Corporal Cockwell became chief ruler in the Synagogue of H.Q.'s, after the most strenuous efforts and these efforts included the overthrow of Bombardier Fred Letheren, fresh from Shorncliffe and a too-fast signaller. The latter is a member of the now famous "Daw-de-Daw" family. We believe that, in their own family circle, they talk in Morse Code only and their Coat-of-Arms is a pair of flags rampant on a background of blue. Some escutcheon! Then Corporal Cockwell was promoted some thought he walked up and down in front of the Order board on which promotions were printed and stood in front of it too long, looking for congratulations but in any case Cockwell put it over Letheren, the Shorncliffe Instructor.

We lost some good men and gained some good ones in the interchange with the Divisional Ammunition Column (D.A.C.). There was a feeling that Sergeant Wilson should have stayed where he was and that Mr. Crowe, even if he did pull a boner taking the battery into action, should have stayed with the battery.Then Corporal MacMillan appeared on the skyline, and remarked soberly the first time he went into the cook-house, "there's that bread loafing around again".

We have with us the Kinnie brothers, "Sunday" and "Grouch," as a result of the change. Did you ever notice the number of long streaks who came into the battery from the column - Teasdale, McGillivray, Archibald, Brackett and the others - "Fish Eaters" and "Spud Islanders" to a man, nourished in a hungry country and the salt sea air.

You will think often of experiences in Godalming and in Guildford - of the girl you took up the river, of the day you and your chum spent at Guildford with the two that you picked up on the bicycles. Someone says "No! no!" looking at the old castle. But it is quite true. Ask General Service Wilson and John D. Rottensmeller if it is not true. The night you would have risked an extra guard or picket, a trip on the carpet, and anything else, to see the girl you wanted to see and who wanted to see you; the night you came forging home in a fast taxi or an open car with the wind surging through your ears, and the driver bribed to exceed all known speed limits, so that you might be back in time for roll-call. It was because Bombardier Copeland failed to make it snappy on one of these trips that he reverted to the ranks. Lautenslayer, on the other hand, had several all-night trips and got away with it every time. Smooth old Lottie!

As for Johnny Porteous, he used to tumble into bed at night, in bandolier, spurs, and everything complete but he was first to be up the next morning and never turned a hair. "Working this morning", he used to say to Tex Snyder as Tex struggled with a recalcitrant horse trying to get him shod. "Why, man, ye're sweating; Ha! Ha! Ye ain't supposed to work in King George's Army. Why I never work. I'm ridin' instructor, Ha! Ha! Had a drink this mornin'? I had a drink o' whiskey, Ha! Ha!" Fletcher and Corporal Algie used to make echoes ring in C Sub at night after an evening out and would come staggering out on parade next morning, Fletcher with his nose curling up and Algie with a dark brown look on his face.

To turn to the romance of the thing, they say that Hector Cowan is going back some day to a little village called Eashing, and that Cupid almost scored a touch-down on him there. In any case he made good use of his time while Jack Doherty entertained the old folks with discussions on the value of a University education. Jack never loses sight of the fact that he is a "Varsity" man. Hec thinks very highly of the damsel because of the fact that, on parting, the old folks tried to make a formal farewell of it but she found she had forgotten to say something to Hec and went out to tell him at the garden gate. Happily Sergeant Hill was never awake long enough at a time to know how often "Hec" got away from him to go to his lady-love.

The day on which King George gave the division "the once over" on Hankley Comon (July 1st)was valuable simply because it got the whole Battery by the cars over the question, "Was he mounted or dismounted?" There are still lots of men who say he was both and neither but whether he was or not, he thought we were good enough for France and at noon on July 13th we left the gun-park for the last time, going to Milford station en route for Southampton. Salvoes of cheers greeted us everywhere and we knew we were off this time.

From Southampton we went to Le Havre, from Le Havre to Point "3", from Point "3" by train to Godewaersvelde in Belgium and climbed down within sound of the guns at last. The French and Belgian children sang the Marseillaise and cried "Pennee! Pennee!" while the gendarmes grinned and made the sign of throat cutting. Clearly this was the land where they murdered each other and thought nothing of it.

In France

The movements in France are naturally divided by the half-dozen positions which the Battery has taken up on various parts of the front. Sergeant-Major Bob Purvis commenced to warn the men as soon as he got them to France. In his historic speech delivered to the troops behind a barn "somewhere in France", he delivered himself as follows: "Youse men are in the war zone now. Up to now you've just been playing at the game. Today you commence soldiering in - earnest" - and each man worth his salt has been soldiering in earnest ever since; but before we had been in the Ypres salient very long, the "S.M." was hunting for a bomb-proof dugout in every hole along the railroad dugouts!

Now that Ypres salient was not a specially healthy spot, as all the Nos.1 who took a trip to the front line "O-Pipping" were quite ready to admit. They were curious to get there and just as curious to get back to the Battery. I have this from as reliable Nos.1 as our present Sergeant-Major (Buss) and Sergeant Mutchmor. It was there that Harry Chace, that dashing Mail orderly, claimed to have had a guy's brains spattered over his boot and they may be there yet for all Harry cares. He has had some far more hair-raising experiences since then; little wonder they can him "Hairbreadth Harry"!

There was the Belgian Battery behind us. Their system was to fire away all their ammunition and then sit tight until the next call, "Ze Belgian Battery vill prepare to bombard" and they did. There was the shell that struck B Sub

-gun-pit- a 5.9 at least - and the one that got Cooke's dug-out - when Cooke was out, unfortunately. Fritz was after the officers too, and sent them scuttling to safer quarters on the double. Charlie Flesch stood cussing in broken English amongst the ruins of his cook-house and the latrines went toppling over.

Conroy, one of the Spud Islanders, could tell you about the shrapnel shower around Sanctuary Wood; and I don't suppose there was a man who went up to the front by way of Zillebeke St., Maple Copse, Sanctuary Wood, Davidson Lane, and Winnipeg Street who did not wish himself elsewhere at times. Lieutenant Cockburn was the only man who kept his head up - but he always keeps his head up anywhere. They say he would stretch out a dainty finger and pick the shrapnel bullet out of the wall of the trench, and it has just missed him at that. Pretty cool girl, our Clara! What! They say that Harold Grant Masson chased a rat over the parapet the first day up; but Masson himself says, "My Gad! What a yarn! Cripe Almighty!"

Old "Weary" Beatty should be able to tell us something about the Ypres salient if his tongue has got the double-kink out of it by now. When Ralph Connor met Weary casually one day at Don 10, he passed the time of day and politely offered Weary a good cigarette. "A Hell of a war!" said Weary, with his mouth full as usual; but "Fritz" had the wind up "Weary's" back. Still, he got the nice "Blighty" he had always wanted and took it sitting down. It would be interesting to know if he ever got rid of that Infantry Commission which he has been trying to lose for a while, and what he thinks now of "the great European conflict in which we are engaged."

But if you wish to have a really racy account of the doings in the famous salient go to Fred Letheren of the "Daw-de-Daw" family. He will tell you, with a very free use of G-damning and other oaths, of the narrow escapes he had in Peter Street and how Cockwell put it over him. Or you may ask Gunner (and ex-telephonist) Fowke, at present holding down a position of trust on the cook-house staff. He will tell you how the Ypres salient made him the mental, moral and physical wreck which you can now plainly see he now is. Ask him if he remembers coming down from the front-line in the face of our own barrage, the morning Fritz tried to come over on Hill 60.

But the worst of it was that we left a man at Ypres when we pulled out of there - old "Bush" Downie, one of the happiest and cheeriest fellows who ever stood on parade in this Battery. As we left the Poperinghe horse-lines behind, on a certain rainy morning and thought of that half-circle of flares going up at night around the salient, the thought came also, of a neat brown cross in the grave-yard behind Transport Farm just in front of the muzzle of the guns and on it these words, "Killed in Action, Gunner K.B. Downie - Blessed are the pure in heart for they shall see God."

In the salient we were under fire for the first time. In war pictures one expects to see wrecked wagons, dead horses, half-buried corpses and farms crumbling under shell-fire. We saw them all there and we will never forget it. It would be better if we could.

Rest Camp

Now, if there is one thing more than another that this Battery (in my observation) hates, it is rest camps. As we ride into a rest camp, you can see the hostile look appearing on the face of Old Ben Case. The story goes that "Cap" Donald once called him "an eye-sore to the Battery", and Ben is proud of the distinction. So as we go into the rest camp lines you hear Ben say, "Pretty rotten." "What, Ben?", you ask. "This regimental stuff," he answers, "Shining buttons, cleaning of clothes, and shining boots. Parades, too," he adds, with a bitter look. "It is kind of rotten," you say in sympathy. "Your blinking right it is," says Ben, using language which is not according to Hoyle.

Because of this Regimental stuff, we will pass over the Watou lines where we used to go around "the square" first thing in the morning on the dead gallop and where Sergeant-Major Purvis was jumped on by the Divisional Commander for having a dirty saddle. Bombardier Lautenslayer brought down the house in the big barn one night when he came home from Watou with that popular song half-made. It goes -

"Keep your harness burnished
The — — I will furnish

Groom your horses till they shine
You rah-rah College boys,
There's no silver lining
Through the dark cloud lining
I've got the hump,
And I'll make you jump
Till we all go home"

The man who had got the "hump" was our old friend Bob Purvis.

We will pass on after two references, one to Major Irving who used to sleep in his mess-cart Charlie Flesch reported gleefully one morning after a rainy night, "The blinkingst major schlept all night in his blinkingst mess-cart. It is vet as a — — ."

Another reference is to the day we pulled out of these lines without dinner. The Major was anxious to be at the rendezvous on time and Bob Purvis could not summon up enough nerve to report to him that he neglected to tell the cook to have dinner early. When the Fall-In blew, the boys were still lined up. Orders came to dump the dixies but some drivers who were nervy enough to take their dinner, ate it; others took it and ran, while others went off hungry and in a hostile mood.

We will pass over both Kemmel positions, which were so homelike. We did nothing there but pick blackberries and wander around over Kemmel Hill. There was no war on there at all. The cows used to pasture in front of the guns. Can you beat it! We were only about a week in each place anyway.

So now we pass along down the long road to the Somme on October 3rd.

The Somme

There was something like a war! The first time we came out on the plain and saw the town of Albert in the hollow beneath us with the Ancre flowing through it and the Golden Virgin with the child in her arms shining from the Cathedral, the big guns were pounding away towards Thiepval, and the first night we went into action, the guns and wagons got stuck in the mud which was anything from a foot to four feet deep.

You may know how serious a war it was when I remind you that Major Irving was killed 100 yards in front of the first battery position, after we had been there three days - a curious, abrupt man, full of strange notions and with a remote English way. He was an unapproachable man but a good soldier and an efficient artilleryman with a keen eye for slackers and swift to con-

demn slip-shod work. There was regret and pity in every man's heart as they saw him lying there so thin and worn, pale and lifeless on the stretcher.

All were impressed but Charlie Flesch. "It is var. It may happen to every von of us," said Charlie, as he raised his hand in a final way. "In dis var it iss shtiffs all der time and der wounded." "And dis does not go to Svayne" he added, swinging a sack with certain valuables belonging to the Major's in it. "Dere is a vatch here. Der is money No, dis does not go to Svayne. Dis goes to the head officer of der blinkingst battery."

Something like a war there all right when it got Clara Cockburn's goat and sent him to hospital, wounded and shell-shocked!!! To quote his own words, which he used while sitting quietly - very quietly in a certain section of Gilbert Alley, which was anything but a health resort, "This is a hell of a place!" Gone was all his old sang-froid and his head actually drooped. You see Fritz tried to register on him and Teasdale and Kay as they walked along the Bapaume road. The way the three of them took to the ditch was a revelation. But that was too much for Clara.

The drivers will tell you the same story, for their experiences so far are- (1) cleaning harness, and (2) going over the ridge at the Somme with ammunition, under shell-fire. That was in the second position to the left of Martinpuich. Corporal Wilson, Andy Lane, and Bert MacKay can all tell how close they came to passing in their checks. If there is anything in this predestination stuff, then the good Lord must be grooming these men down for big jobs. Corporal Wilson had his horse (Old Dynamite) killed beneath him and, when "G.S." stood up all he could see was the face of J.J. Greenlee looking over the edge of a shell-hole with eyes like saucers and signaling frantically for him to come over. As it was "Dode" got a piece through the rim of his steel helmet and went home with his heart thumping like a trip-hammer, telling the boys that he really ought not to be there at all, but pushing up daisies back on the ridge. Bert MacKay was saved by something in his tunic and Andy Lane got off with a piece in his arm.

Talk about your story books and pictures! It had them all beaten. To see these wagons and teams struggling over the ridge, just on the sky-line, with the shells splashing amongst them, the earth shooting up in great columns and the drivers flailing away at the teams with their whips.

It was at the Somme that Chuck Lawrence, known also as "Chud"or "Long Shot", distinguished himself by shinnying up a tree on the Bapaume Road, schoolboy fashion, and we have every reason to believe he won a bet from Mr. Youell, to the effect that the latter could not climb the tree without the aid of a ladder. It was a sight to see Chuck winding himself two or three times around the trunk of that tree when a Fritzie plane came over and started spraying bullets around the neighborhood.

It was at the Somme that Earache Eating Bingham sat down suddenly in a mud hole in the front line and came home with the better part of Death Valley on his boots and pants. This is the same Bingham who is known variously as "Brigadier, Bandolier, Bombardier" Bingham, also as "the Shrimp" and "the Louse".

It was at the Somme that the Rev. James Niven McPhail wakened up one morning in the telephone-pit to find himself lying in about three inches of water, and said, like a dainty lady who has soiled her skirts, "Tut! tut! tut! dear! dear! dear! I'm in an awful mess." And Teasdale, being awakened out of dewy sleep to do his shift on the telephone, declared, "Damn telephone! As bad as a baby! Needs somebody to look after it all the time! Ought to have a nurse!"

Oh! it was great to be rolled up in the blankets at night and hear those big "homesteaders" come droning up the valley through the mist or to see them shooting the dirt sky-high on the ridge behind the guns or on the ridge in front. Jimmy Kingsburgh had often to leave the meals half-cooked and hike to a flank; then come back to find dirt and corruption over everything. But in spite of smoke and mud and shell-fire, Jimmy's meals were always more tasty than any the other cooks made.

The way the 43rd eased themselves in on the Somme scrap and out again is a story well worth telling. We say Lautenslayer go down the line with a piece of H.E. in his knee and a smile on his face. We have never seen him since although the savour of his stories and his songs and his conversation still lingers amongst the old-timers. Fred Letheren got shell-shocked but he was well enough to be able to tell the boys who were pouring rum down his throat how he-had-found-a-a-a German Ger-German buckle and what a good souvenir it was. Andy Anderson, the minister's son, being induced to go to Martinpuich one day for timber got a piece of H.E. in his chest and the point is that by rights Kay should have got it as the shell landed nearer him than it did Anderson. Oh! We were a lucky battery at the Somme all right for the Observation Post was blown in on the same day that we pulled out - the day no one went up.

As some of us rode down the road to Albert in a wagon, we thought of many things such as the collapse of Clara's nerve, the famous crossing of the Bapaume road; the morning that Letheren, Case, Conroy, Kay and Clara lay in the shell holes in front of the Sugar Refinery while Fritz scorched the ground all around. We thought of Le Sars and of Courcelette, of Martinpuich and of Pozieres, of Gilbert Alley and of the Mule Track, but we thought also of the Major, who had drilled us into shape and who knew better than any of his officers how to register a gun, being carried down the valley, limp and cold, with the blue pallor of death from H.E. on his thin face.

Maroeuil

And now we have come to this place, after having been in the Big Push front from October 9th till November 26th and long enough too! In this chalk country close to the famous "Labyrinth" things are quieter. We now have for the first time the luxury of a narrow-gauge railway to bring up ammunition and the drivers have nothing to do but clean harness. All the college chaps and would-be heroes have given up all idea of taking up open positions and dashing into positions under shell fire! They have given up these ideas and settled down to grooming horses, cleaning harness and drinking wine or coffee at the nearest Estaminets. The gunners are quite resigned to slugging ammunition, doing gun-guards, and acting as air scout or battery orderly, or brigade orderly, or spare fatigue artist. It seems a weary war as we come along to Christmas this Year.

We are a battery of characters if we could only see ourselves. There is Sergeant-Major Buss, who has learned from the fact that Bob Purvis came back to the ranks with a bump, just how far a Sergeant-Major may go. There is "Iodine" King, whom Scotty MacLean is always looking for. There is Johnny Porteous, who is quite reconciled to being called "Boo-Boo, Bombproofer." There is Sergeant Briggs who refused to be Quarter-Master's Assistant, who set his jaw and went back to the guns. There is Quarter-Master Sergeant George Brown Ball (reverence his grey hairs) who has weathered many a storm and seems to be able to hold down his job. He is called "Old Indent" and his greatest fun is to call the Rev. Driver Billy Patton "Old Profanity" and warn him that he will have him up before the General Assembly for his sins.

There is Sergeant Harvey who has the finest job in the British Army. He walks softly and carries a big stick. There is "Shiny A", otherwise Sergeant McMillan, who still makes his old joke about the bread loafing around. There is Corporal Pettitt who is an old enough soldier to be able to see some good in all officers. He has always impressed me by the way he eats his meals. He eats them all faithfully, every scrap goes down. He eats as if he were sitting at the Sacrament. He sits there as a silent rebuke to the "growsers", the discontented and kickers, three or four times a day. But when his horses cut up he can tear off an oath of great power and he can sing a song or drink a glass with the best of them. However, his heart is with his wife and family in Guelph, and he should never have left them.

There is Sergeant Mutchmor who is an awful fellow to argue with officers, and his able Lieutenant, Tubby Turnbull, who is full of Knox College sarcasm. There is Corporal Wilson from the Peace River country who knows a horse from a hole in the ground and takes a horse off the line on which he rides off for distant parts whenever he takes the notion. There is Corporal Coutts, known to all as "Grouch Bill". The way he has A Sub curled around his finger is a sight. Gunner Greenlee has become Bombardier Greenlee, Quarter-Master's Assistant, busy here and there and violently opposed to all stories of a questionable nature. I am sorry to have to record that O.C. Smith, who is "a helluva man" takes advantage of this fact to shoot all the stories he knows when Greenlee is around.

Coming to the men, there is Joshaway Carter (606) who is becoming "'ardened to it". There is Brady Ludgate, ex-railroader who reports on the condition of the roads and can tell you "how many are in" any day. There is Warrener, the comedian, who has a furious appetite and is very happy in his famous lines commencing, "Cab! Lady! Cab!" "No! Not today."There is a Greaser Mullins and skeen the actor, also known as "Caruso, the battery canary". There is little McQuarrie, the human encyclopedia, and Neelands, who is particularly effective in his famous imitation of liquor coming out of a bottle. He can imitate it going back in again, but he always empties it last of all. There is "Nut Bar" or Dunbar, one of the most faithful and hard working men in the battery. In his spare time he writes letters, and worries about his Guelph mail.

There are the Niggers - Knight, Moss and Worth, "the native". There is "Army" Howard, the great Negro sprinter who is "Clara" Cockburn's special favourite and always does any detailing. There is Bombardier McKenzie who will do as Sergeant Crookwell tells him, just as there is his mate, Kay, who will not. McKenzie by the way sits a good saddle and is a nervy cuss. Jimmie Kingsburgh has ceased being "Ginger", Charlie Flesch's assistant, and has become a fully fledged cook. Jack Porteous says - "We're all going to die anyway. It's too damned damp in this country."

Then about the officers. What are we to say about them? Thank the Lord we belong to an army in which we can look the officers in the eye and talk to them and about them without being court-martialed. Sometimes we hate them all, usually at reveille and at parade times, and then a man is apt to hate himself as well. Sometimes we are agreed that they are not half bad but, as a rule, when we sit around the dugout fires, we feel sorry for them because they are forced to put up with one another's society and cannot chum with the rank and file. "Cap" is always the same, but, sometimes, we think he might get up earlier in the morning and show more signs of life. "Clara" is just "Clara" the sort of fellow who will call attention to a man in the ranks as "that man with the funny-colored boots." "Long Shot" Lawrence we think sometimes is not half bad. But others again have an entirely different story and say that he has been getting very snotty lately. "Edgar Pip" Black is President of the Officers' Mess and a regular fellow but it is only fair that he ought to be washed and fully awake when he comes to inspect men and dugouts in the mornings.

And that is all - yes, really and truly, it is absolutely all. I was told to go as far as I liked and I did. Hope I have not gone farther than you liked. What is there left for me to do but wish you all the compliments of the Season?

H.R. Kay,
Aubigny, France.
Christmas, 1916.

I CANT GET 'EM UP
I CANT GET 'EM UP
PICKET
FRISE

Chapter I -2

Y Position, Vimy

September 3rd, 1917

I have tried and tried again to start writing this "dope" in my dugout in the railway bank. You nearly all know what dugout and what railway bank. But it is only now that I have been able to do it. You see I am living with confirmed Bombardier Cooke, who, is also a confirmed hot-air shooter, and with Chief Cook and Dixie Washer, Bill MacNamara, who is a particularly wild Irishman. Just when I was settling down, Acting-Bombardier Flesch, the Salvage King, the Doctor from Vimy, Military Medal, Croix de Guerre, etc., etc., would appear, and start to shout, "I-sack, I-sack, de Yiddisher navy will now bombard mit howitzers, mit eight inch dis time," and at once great lumps of that part of France would commence to arrive in the door of the dugout. Then there would be an outcry from Cooke, who had been disturbed in making out his "Ack" report, or in drafting a rotten "leave" list, and there would be a battle royal outside. Finally, Charlie, "Oh, leave me go, I-sack. Leave me go, kit I haf no vind, no vind at all, kit."

If it was not Charlie and George, then it would be MacNamara singing at the top of his Voice, especially the song commencing:

"When we get to Blighty,
Oh, Lord Almighty!"

If he was not doing this he would be arguing with Cooke about his back-pay, or else trying to prove that "the ould man" (Major Coghlan) would amount to something.

I hope you see what I had to contend with; but you all laughed so heartily at my last spasm, read to you at Aubigny, that I believe almost anything at all will satisfy you, and that you will laugh at anything at all. Let me remind you that there is little or no credit due to me because you were amused on that memorable evening. It was really yourselves who provided the amusement. It was your own wit or your own brave or laughable actions that I read out to you. In laughing so uproariously, you were really laughing at yourselves and at one another.

Still At Maroeuil

When I think of Maroeuil I think of "Lefty" Youell, the Terror of the Sandhills, on the trail of "Old Lizzie," the Fritzie trench-mortar in the Visic Sap, called by some vulgar fellows, "The Physic Sap." Some cynical men declared that Lefty was on the trail of a Military Cross rather than a trench-mortar, and I believe that "Tubby" Turnbull was the leader of a crowd who sincerely hoped that "Lefty" got an R.I.P. In any case, the said "Lefty" took a great liking to F.O.O. work, and, being liaison officer, he trotted around Elbe and Douai and Bentata and Rocade, and all the trenches we know so well, mud to the eyes, with Burns, carrying his (Lefty's) bed, always in the offing. He got Knechtel to make souvenirs for all the infantry officers, and ended up by getting neither "Old Lizzie," nor the Military Medal, nor a R.I.P.

How successful "Lefty" was in handling "Old Lizzie" may be judged from the following story:

"Lefty" is in Visic Sap, and is gazing over the parapet with his short legs stiffened and his stern end in the usual position-hanging out like a signboard. He has already got rid of about 100 rounds, after adding and dropping and switching, firing salvoes, battery fire, gun fire, section fire, and all other kinds of fire. For a time "Lizzie" is quiet, and "Lefty" kids himself along that he has silenced her. He calls up the heavies and turns on a battery of 9.2's on poor old "Lizzie." They tear up the country for several km around, while "Lefty" is beside himself with joy. "Lizzie" finally quiets down. "Lefty" thanks the Adjutant and the Heavies. The Adjutant thanks "Lefty" and the Heavies. The Heavies thank "Lefty" and the Adjutant. "Lefty" thanks Sergeant Crookwell and the linesmen, Kay and Bombardier McKenzie. Everyone goes home in a glow of triumph. Next morning we again visit the sap, and there is "Lizzie" at her old stand, popping them over as usual. Great is the disappointment. "Lefty"swears. "Tubby"Turnbull, as he pulls on his sox in the morning, sums up the situation. "He works hard. He works hard. But what does he do? What does he do? I think he's a poor-r-r tool." And with these few words, "Tubby" proceeds to "louse" himself.

But time was when Major Irving used to have "Lefty" on the jump at Ypres, and actually told him to either find a new target or come in." "Lefty" has more confidence in himself since those days, and has become a tough guy.

But from "Lefty" we turn to McCrudden, whose career with this Battery had been short and feverish. Nobody ever thought when they saw him leading his mob up to dig in trench mortars in what the gunners thought was "No Man's Land," that he would turn out to be the high-explosive person that he has become. After a few confidential talks in the officers' mess, "Tubby" actually believed in him, and said he was a good man. But he was from the battle of Shorncliffe, so what could you expect?

Edgar P. Black, known as "Edgar Pip," used to get up - at times - after he and Tom Hill had sworn at each other for half-an-hour or so, and had a pitched battle with oranges or stones, or books or boots, or whatever happened to be handy. Edgar would play poker all over the country, and return in the morning when the last man on guard was putting on the fire in the cook-house. When it was his turn to be Orderly Officer, old Tom Hill would go and waken him with these words, "When the H— are you gaen tae get up? Do ye no ken ye're Orderly Officer?" Then, after a while, Black would get up and go out to inspect the subs. to see if they were in good shape, being unwashed, unshaven, and in his trench-waders. Clara, now, was quite different. He always looked spic-and-span, and always brought a sweet breath of talcum-powder with him. Lawrence was always Lawrence and nothing more, conscientious to a pin-point, and never having very much fun. "Cap" Donald took things easy, as he usually does, and never worried any more than he could help.

Up at the guns Andy Anderson and Ben Case used to live "beyond the pale of the law" away down the line somewhere; and Andy turned up asking for breakfast one morning just when the cooks were ready to dish up dinner. He was vastly surprised to find out the time of day. Biggs forsook the quartermaster and came back to the guns as a Sergeant. He took all that was left of "D" sub. and licked it into shape in no time with his characteristic vigour. "Nut-bar" (Dunbar) was a physical wreck. "Smittie" (Smith) was the sloppiest man in the outfit, but he had Tom O'Neil to work with - a Shorncliffe recruit - and he is good material.

We all wrestled with Cooke for candles every night, and went to Maroeuil every chance we got. "Old Dope" Richardson, another Shorncliffe draft, went oftener than some, and got all the champagne and other stuff to drink that he could lay his hands on. He and Simpson tried Headquarters, but did not make good. G. S. Wilson insists on calling Simpson, "Simp," just as he calls Dunbar, "Nutbar"; but Simpson found a career open to him in sanitary work, and carried on there.

The Batmen's Association were a very boisterous lot at this gun position - Old "Right-a-vay" Flesch, Bill Swayne (better known as "Corp. Turnover" or Fed-up Swayne), Josh Carter, old Vant (Heinie), "Minnie" Burns, and T. Hill. They all used to go wandering down to Maroeuil, and on a Sunday morning come staggering home. Not drunk! O Lord, no! but just happy. Happy enough to cut all the buttons off old Vant's clothes one night.

Then at the guns we had the Battery songsters - first of whom was Skeen, best known as Caruso, the Battery Canary; "Greaser" Mullins, who warbled night and day; and Corporal Lillow, the lyric tenor, who used to sell good understandings to people in Guelph. The boys used to sit with their mouths open listening to Skeen telling his stories of stage life. "Man! man!" Skeen would say, "perfectly mar-vel-lous. Oh! boy set me down anywhere in little old Noo Yawk, and I won't worry." The boys used to show him pictures of all the actors and actresses, and ask him if he knew them. He knew them all - had met them in Broadway or in 'Frisco or in Chicago. Wonderful man, Skeen; but he offended some of us with his remarks about women!

Now the horse-lines at Maroeuil were pretty Jake, just as the gun-position was pretty bomb-proof. The drivers and bomb-proofers; and artificers and spare gunners were divided into two mobs - (1) those who were admirers of the dark-eyed Helène in the estaminet across the road, and (2) those who followed "the merry widow" in the estaminet where the left section slept. The greater number went to dark-eyed Helène, because she was more frolicsome, and, besides, the soup had more stuff in it over there. Anyway, the fellows all took the soup and drunk up their pay, and in the meantime smiled at Helène, and looked at her and watched her, and sometimes tried to put an arm around her. But she danced out of the way and chased them all out-all except George Harvey and Sergeant-Major Buss.

Why we got so religious there, that we used to even have church parades, with old "Tubby" Turnbull, and "Grouch" Bill Coutts, and Reverend Driver Patton-Leadswinger, Old Profanity, etc., - as preachers. "Tubby" turned out one Sunday with his hair slick and a put-upon look about him. It looked to be a heavy duty for "Tubby." He had no chew in his mouth at the time, as there was no chance to spit there. Now that he is gone, we will never forget "Tubby's" opening sentences: "I don't know that I'm very fit to conduct a religious service," said he. "If smoking and chewing tobacco, and pulling off an oath now and then makes a man wicked, then I am a pretty bad character" - this with a downcast look. But "Tubby" was right there with his college sermon just the same, and a flow of language which made George Cooke sound like a man who had a hesitation in his speech.

Bill Coutts, they say, put up a good speel; but Billy Patton was the man who took the fancy of the boys, with his address on Solomon and his many wives all under one roof. It was General Mitchell who put a crimp in the religious life of the horse-lines. Bombardier Greenlee was slated to speak, but the General put his foot down, and we never heard that address.

The Little Preacher

"These college guys has queered this here battery," said big "Nigger" Jim Moss, the limber gunner, with heavy emphasis. Big Jim tipped the scales at over 250 lbs., and was called "Nigger Jim" because of his fondness for

imitating the soft nigger drawl, and a supposed resemblance to the blacks from the torrid zone.

"Now, Jim, I just naturally won't stand for anything against 'Tubby' Turnbull," said Brady Ludgate. "He may be a blamed preacher, but he knows a bee from a bull's foot. Can't put much over on old 'Tubby,'" went on Brady. "Remember how they tried to stick it over him on that job of digging in trench-mortars. He stood up to old 'Cap' Donald on that, and got away with it, too. Great boy, our 'Tubby,'" concluded Brady, as he slouched away with the unmistakable gait of a railroader.

'Well, what I wants to know is this," persisted "Nigger" Jim. "Will old 'Tubby' quit bein' a preacher when he goes back to God's country? He smokes, he chews, he swears sometimes. Now, how about it?" he asked, with a puzzled expression on his big brown face.

"And what have you to say against 'Busy B?'" Mutchmor, the Sergeant, who had been lying on a bank watching the fortunes of a "Fritzie" plane under fire from our "Archies," now joined the group - a big tireless worker, with a passion for detail, he had the confidence of all ranks, and earned his promotion by sweating for it.

This question being the signal for a friendly sparring match about the efficiency of the various subsections, the light of battle shone in each eye.

"'Busy B's' got nothin' on 'Shiny A'"- this from Mullins, the loud-talking limber-gunner of that subsection, who went by the name of "Greaser" Mullins. "Good old 'Shiny A'" came in a rousing chorus from many throats, as "Greaser' Mullins raised his right hand as a signal.

"And what gun put 'Old Lizzie' out of action?" said Neelands of C sub, who used to be a sergeant, and was popularly known as "the five thousand-dollar engineer," mainly because he had attended a school for practical science, and spent his spare time trailing spare meridians in the north country. "Old Lizzie" was the huge German-mortar which had pounded up the front line for days, and defied all efforts to locate her hiding-place.

"Come on, 'Dirty D,'" said a taunting voice in an effort to rouse the anger of the crew of No. 4 gun. "Well, she's the most accurate gun of the lot," said Bombardier MacKay quietly, looking up in a half-shy way. MacKay seldom swore, and was known to carry a copy of Browning's poems in his haversack.

"Used to be C sub gun until we left the last position" said little McQuarrie, by way of a come-back. McQuarrie's comebacks were famous. He was called the walking encyclopedia, and had all the facts at his finger ends.

"Well, old 'Tubby's' a good man, anyway, even if he is a preacher," said Neelands, returning without warning to the former subject.

"Well, who says he's not?" came defiantly from Mutchmor, who always boosted the men of his sub, and in particular Turnbull, who was his best gunner and his Bombardier as well. "You ought to hear him speel, too," he added, looking away over the white chalk ridge before the guns.

"Regular midway artist, I guess," said Brady Ludgate.

"You bet," replied Mutchmor. "Some little speeler; and you should get a chance to hear him speak on Sunday. They say 'Old Lefty Lou' has rung him in to take service next Sunday at the horse-lines."

"'Lefty Lou's' another of these college men," said "Nigger" Jim, beetling his eyebrows.

"Battery Action!" came from the telephone pit, and instantly the social group of N.C.O's and men radiated from a common centre towards the four gun-pits.

Crossing The Ridge

After the big attack on the ridge the Battery lay out of action for several days-and they were anxious days for us. Other batteries beside us were moving forward, packing with feverish haste, strapping kits and equipment on the limbers - but still we lay inactive. It was true a few favoured ones amongst us had been up and looked over the ridge. We had seen our own shells splashing up the dirt at certain points in the promised land, but the order came to cease firing, as our patrols were now through the village of V—-, so the guns lay silent in the pits, and the gunners just mooned about waiting for something to happen.

Then came "McCrudden's Expeditionary Force," as we called it. On ten minutes notice ten of us were warned to go with Lieut. H.E. McCrudden on an advance party, to occupy a new position over the ridge, in the village of Vimy. So off we went in single file, up by the twin craters, and across what used to be No Man's Land on the top of the ridge.

What observation he had! - a clear sweep for miles on every side. But there was no halting around there, so down we went across the wide valley, with the wreck of an aeroplane lying crumpled in a corner. A stern, Scotch voice ordered us off the road, which went edging down one side of the valley, and we knew that Fritz still had a few guns ranging on that spot. McCrudden had the "wind up," and we made a wide detour, but the valley opened out, and almost at once we came on broken limbers and dead horses. Poor old Fritz! he "got his" in backing out from there. At dusk our single file came to a halt behind a hedge on the edge of the village, and we scattered to look for quarters. It was then that I first saw the cellar and marked it for occupation.

Five Men In A Cellar

"Hullo, Headquarters! Breakfast up in ten minutes," yelled a raucous voice, and a stick beat a smacking tattoo on the brick wall.

Absolute silence.

"Hullo, down there, you linesmen! Don't make it a bloomin' lifetime either."

"All ri'!" came the sleepy reply.

"This cellar for orderly officer, 'tion," continued the voice, and the guard scrambled down the stone steps. "Headquarters fellahs 'ud sleep all day if you'd let 'em," said Ludgate; but he spoke to five mutes, and peered into the darkness hopefully.

I turned lazily and saw the ruddy face of the ex-railroader framed in the patch of light at the bottom of the stairway. "Hullo, Brady," said I, "how's she goin' this morning -"

"Well, nearly!" was the cryptic reply.

"Many in to-day?" was my next effort - for the boys from old Ontario never forge the familiar, inevitable question addressed by the storekeeper in their native town to Old Josh or William Walter who have driven in for the day.

"Just a few! Roads pretty bad," said Brady. Then coming back to present conditions, "No! not many in; Fritz shellin' the roads"- and at that moment we all heard a crash somewhere above which told its own story.

"Any landing very adjacent?" said a muffled voice, which came from "Weary" Beattie.

"Ha! ha! ha!" yelled Brady, yelling like a wild hyena. "Beaucoup overhead traffic this morning, 'Weary.' Wish you were in Pembroke, `Weary?'"

"You're bloomin' right," said "Weary," now fully, awake, but unwilling to get up. "Well, don't make it a lifetime," said Brady, as he rose from the steps. "This here battery can't wait all day."

"What's for breakfast?" I shouted to his vanishing figure.

"Punk and pig, mush and Sergeant-Major's tea," came the reply, which, being interpreted, means bread, bacon, porridge and tea a little more bitter than usual.

"Whose turn is it to get breakfast?" demanded Teasdale, for whom all the bunks were too short, and whose feet were always in the way.

"I got it yesterday," came incisively from Old Ben Case, who spoke in the tone of a man who, washing his hands of the whole business, could not be detailed on any pretext.

"Well, I got supper last night," I began in self-defence.

"Well, but a dinner isn't the same as a breakfast," urged Ben, who was the best arguer amongst us, and had been known to argue with a Colonel, to the confusion of that notable.

"How about you, Teasdale?" said Anderson, the minister's son, being heard for the first time.

"Another county heard from," said I. "Why, he just came off shift on the telephone at four o'clock this morning."

"Yes, and nearly got napooed coming over from the telephone-pit," said Teasdale. "Gas shells falling all over. Gee!" he continued, in his brief, telegraphic way. "H—- of a war! Wish I was home."

"Poor old McTavish doesn't have much fun," said the minister's son, who always insisted on calling our friend McTavish, for some obscure reason.

"Not so much of the poor old McTavish," came from Case's corner. "If you think he isn't a good man, you're crazy. Why, man, he's had a course. He's a Class A man." We never forgot that Teasdale was a qualified signaller and could receive and send messages on the Fullerphone.

"Well, I'd rather be a linesman than a bloomin' telephonist, any day," said I. "This crawling out on shift at all hours of the night gets my goat."

"You bet cher life," said Teasdale, and stretched himself contentedly in his bunk, when, "Holy Mackinaw! keep your blank-blankety-blanked feet out of my face," shouted Old Ben, who slept with his head next to that worthy's feet.

"Sorry, Ben," was the reply, for the owner of the feet was a gentle spirit and a pacifist, his height and bulk to the contrary.

"Well, this won't get us any breakfast," said I, scrambling out from my bunk beneath Anderson and putting out an old Toronto Globe to keep my feet off the cold, tiled floor.

"Well, Scotland, do you think you'll ever amount to anything?" said Andy, whose spirits rose in proportion as he saw prospects of breakfast and of himself lying in bed to eat it.

"Not if this bloomin' war keeps up," I replied, using his own reply, which was a standing joke in the Battery.

"Guess you're a good man," I went on, by way of giving him a chance for his equally famous reply, which was always, "Better than the average, but you ought to see my father," implying that he was good, his father was specially good; in short, that if he was a man, his father might be fairly considered to be a superman.

"Guess you're gonna get breakfast for once, Scotland," added my tormentor.

"First thing you know, I'll get back into bed again and not get it at all," said I, struggling into an Army boot. Loud laughter. "Remember the time at the Maroeuil position, Andy; you came round at noon looking for breakfast when the cooks were getting dinner," said I.

"Poor old Andy, that ought to hold you for a while"- this from Teasdale.

"In the next war," said Anderson, "I am going to be a bomb-proofer-batman to the Brigadier."

By this time I had scrambled up the cellar steps and taken a look around. It was a glorious morning, a clear bright sky, and the air vibrating with the constant hum of aeroplanes. Across the roadway, in the orchard, our neighbours, the 6-inch Howitzers, were sitting on their haunches beneath the trees, heavy with apple blossom; their muzzles were turned toward heaven, and they were barking out defiance at the Bosche batteries. As I looked up the village street towards the square several rounds of enemy fire went crashing home, sending brick-dust high in the air in reddish clouds. Suddenly the range lengthened, and two rounds went sizzling over the roof of the house, bursting with a resounding crash just beyond our gun-pits. I looked down the street, noting the ruined houses and the new shell-holes made the night before. The breeze brought me the faint odour of the gas from the Boche gas-shells of the night, and mingled with it the smell of the dead horse which was killed on the slope of the street two weeks ago and half buried amongst the bricks. The swallows, which have nests above the doorway, were flitting in and out above my head, twittering happily, and there came to my ears from many places three warning whistles.

Gathering up the mess-tins and a pail in which we drew tea for the crowd, I scuttled up the street amongst the debris and shell-holes to the cook-house, which was on the lee-side of a brick wall. Five minutes later I was back, carefully balancing many mess-tins. "First and last call for breakfast," I sang out.

"Say, Hugh, they tell me there's a war on," said a voice, which I knew for "Weary" Beatty's.

"Well, just what you would notice."

"'There's nothing half so sweet in life as love's young dream.'" This from Case, apropos of nothing in particular.

"Some say 'good old Scotland,'" declared Anderson in a challenging voice, "and others again have an entirely different story."

"That's all right - that's all right, Andy; sit up and eat, don't be a dope all your life."

But Anderson was now awake and irrepressible. "Let us now join in the general confession," said he in a lugubrious tone; "come on, Scotland."

"Almighty and most merciful Father, we have all erred and strayed like lost sheep."

"Ah! Oui!" came the response.

"And there is no health in it," continued the quavering voice, jumping to the next part he knew.

"Cut it out! Now, you guys, that's sacreligion," shouted Case; "at least that's what 'Pip Dawn' calls it." Now, "Pip Dawn" was a signaller's nickname for P.D., the initials of our Sergeant, who had a way of mishandling words.

Ben took up the tea-pail, raised it aloft, and said dramatically, as he sat up in the blankets -

"He gave me half-a-pint of water green,
It was crawling and it stunk,
But of all the drinks I've drunk
I'm gratefullest for one from Gungerdeen."

Suddenly there was a crash overhead, and the bricks came cascading down the steps, together with fine dust and smoke. There was a moment's silence. Then every man sprang for his clothes.

"Where are you going, Hughie?"

"Six-inch position, Andy; behind the crest for mine."

Teasdale wound on his puttees. He never went without them. Another shell went screaming overhead.

"He added on that one, don't you think, Hugh? Next one may be ours."

Next one came and went. It was not ours.

"Well, the next one," said Andy, with a nervous laugh.

"Think you'll ever amount to anything, Andy?"

"Not in a place like this."

"What would Mabel say if she could see you now?"

"To H— with her!" was the reply, as he scrambled upstairs, and in five minutes the cellar was clear.

Now the village of Vimy consists of two parts, a higher and a lower. The line which separates the two is made by a ridge which runs the whole breadth of the village. On the west side the ridge is sufficiently pronounced to be a decided escarpment, and behind this natural protection the six-inch howitzers had dug in. From their dugouts in the bank it was possible to get a grand-stand view of the lower village. It was to these dugouts that we now ran. Teasdale, the cigarette smoker, was out of breath and panting painfully.

"Gosh! look at that," said Ben; "just got out in time," and, as we looked, there was a loud detonation and the old ruined house was lost in clouds of smoke and brick-dust. Another struck beside the road and set up the 6-inch charges.

"Holy Mackinaw!" came in a gasp from Andy, "can you beat that!"- as the charges went up in sheets of flame, and 6-inch shells went off with loud explosions. Even at 200 yards we could feel the heat.

The gunners, who had just come in from serving the hows., surveyed the spectacle coldly.

"If you're a blinkin' fool and wants to be a bloomin' 'ero, out yer go and save old 'Lizzie,' said one bloke to his chum.

"You think I'm gone barmy?" said this chum; "not 'arf, I ain't. Besides, I ain't an 'ero, I'm a soldier, I am," thus calling attention to the distinction so often made in this way.

But now the "Boche" gunners had lengthened the range and reached back to the battery in the orchard. We knew every inch of the ground. We knew just where the gun-pits were, where the telephone-pit was, where the covered trench was which ran from the officers' cook-house at the street to the first gun-pit. We knew that it was full of wires connecting us with our own brigade, with the infantry headquarters, and with other batteries, and, worse still, we knew that the deep dugout in the centre would at this very moment be crowded with men. As we heard each shell come screaming over, and saw it fall like a descending baseball within an area so congested with life and so crowded with costly equipment, we felt that each shell seemed to be going to hurt us. As it landed and detonated, and sent up a crater of fresh dirt, etc., we cringed. As the duds landed heavily, sending up spouts of dirt 150 feet high, we cringed. It was not fear that made us cringe, but rather the thought of what damage might be done in such a vital area. It was as if a passive martyr shrank from a thrust at his vitals.

And the men! In the comparatively regular intervals an odd few, who had business to do, could be seen dashing across to safety, or, when they misjudged the interval, scrambling into convenient shell-holes. How puny these scrambling humans seemed to be as they squirmed in their efforts to escape death and dismemberment by high explosives! It seemed to me for a fleeting moment that the only God was Caliban, and that our brave men were the victims of his whims.

"Five-nines, I guess," said Anderson.

"No bon, no bon for the troops!" declared "Weary." "Some say good old Fritz, but I say d——d old Fritz."

"Lord! Ben, you're a tough-looking soldier," said I. "You're half-dressed, unwashed, unshaven, and half-awake. You're not very fussy at any time though, Ben, are you?"

"No! No!" came, the reply, and Ben's face took on the pale cast of thought. "I'm pretty much like my father in many ways. He very seldom brushed his coat or pressed his pants, and neither do I. He hardly ever cleaned his boots or combed his hair, and neither do I. Oh! never wore garters either. Funny, you know."

So Ben gave us his confession of faith as relating to dress while the shells kept screaming over and dropping just in the arena in front of us. At times there would be a pause. Then over they would come again, and the flying pieces would be singing and whining around the dugouts. Some scared us by dropping on the ridge behind us. As things tapered off, Andy declared that he thought he could find it in his heart to go and hunt for some rhubarb in the gardens to the right. "I'm with you, Andy," declared Ben, and off they went.

PART II

Chapter II - 1

Ohlain, Christmas 1917

In appreciation of our dear friend, Hugh Kay, this work which he so cleverly produced is to be taken up, as best we can, from the day when he laid down his pen and went forth to do his duty, never again to return to our midst.

We all respected him for his manly life and his fearlessness in danger - "I am not afraid to die for my King and country" was his spirit - and loved him for his honest heart and his droll tongue, which brought laughter to our lips but left no sting or rankle behind. His account of the doings of this Battery of ours is full of humour, and portrays the salient characteristics of his friends as he saw them in daily intercourse. That he understood human nature, and knew how to describe what he saw, admits of no question.

Kay was a man who knew his duty and did it, and in leaving him behind in a strange land we all felt that something good had passed out of our lives. But we are the better for having known him, for of such men are empires built and the old world made worth while.

It is no small task to have his mantle fall upon one, and this has been rendered doubly difficult, by the advent of what is now known as our "Left (behind) Section," fresh from Shorncliffe, and all with wire in their hats and quite ready to take up positions in the open, tell off for gun-drill or perform any and all of the martial stunts as taught in the months one wastes in Blighty. To get to know and understand these newcomers would take longer time than we have had together, though many of them proved their right to belong to the 43rd by their faithful work in the "hell fire at Kansas Cross and Abraham Heights." When they first arrived and we were informed of this addition to our strength, we were somewhat puzzled, for, at first, we saw nothing before us. Then we lowered our angle of sight, leveled the bubble and discovered a swarm of tiny specimens of humanity wearing an exceedingly jaunty and confident air and greatcoats far too large for them. "Just the type of drivers I brought over with the 29th" remarked our Sergeant-Major through his moustache, "far better than those big drivers we have now."

ERISE
Mont St. Eloi
Tower

"How the hell are they going to load packs on those long-legged mokes?" asked an old-timer, but the Sergeant-Major had espied an individual who seemed to lack employment and was after him in a flash with the time-honoured query, "What are you on?" So the discussion ended.

All through the strenuous summer months, when we, single-handed, held the Ridge against the foe, and usually with only two guns in action at that, we had been hearing vague rumours or "latrine gossip" as the more refined call it. We were going to the 4th Division; we were going to be split up and the Right Section was going to the 9th Battery while the Left was booked for the 21st. We were so highly prized that Colonel Stewart was determined to have us in his famous "flying brigade"; we were going to have 30 pounder guns with a range of 15,000 yards and horse-lines at the base. In fact everyone who came up from the lines had a new tale to unfold. Meantime, we carried on, though "stormed at by shot and shell," and despite the loss of many of our best friends. We nearly lost George Cooke as well, for a musical fragment buried itself in the wall close to his summer cottage and grazed his arm en route. For this he had a month's rest and so had we! During his absence the Salvage King went on his glorious way unchecked, except when by Brady Ludgate. Charlie even went so far as to, resurrect an old howitzer and presented it to, "C" Sub, who had been out of action so often that it was getting past a joke. His fondness for roaming away from the shelter of the railroad track was not shared by many of us, who preferred a quiet life to a noisy death.

Our good friend Sergeant Biggs being away on leave in Paris, his crew under the direction of W.C. "Pip", Curzon, of whom Tom O'Neil remarked that "he would make a fair gunner in time," contrived to, put "D" Sub gun out of action about once a week. Finally, when they fired the ancient weapon, one gunner, armed with a bar - Johnson, had to stand at the mouth of the pit and ram the cases out with great vigor. This did not tend to rapid firing, so they gave up the unequal struggle and decided to give Bill Sharpe a good long holiday at Ordnance.

It was in this position also, that Dunc Irvine's terrific flow of profanity was the cause of his military career being shadowed until such time as the Lord had mercy upon us and took the "ould man" away from us and deposited him in Blighty. Dunc had been called out one day just when old Mac had dished up one of his memorable dinners, and, when he was told to stand down without firing at all, his feelings gave way. "What terrible language," remarked "Dugout Dick" to one of his henchmen, and Dunc's downfall was assured. Now he is coming into his own again. No more will we have to register with Charge IV and Charge V on the same target, or be informed that

the traverse should remain at zero while we move the trail every time the gun jumps off the posts. No more shall the treacherous Boche shake and tremble in his dug-out, as he wonders where the 43rd is going to drop the next one!

During our holding of the Ridge it became necessary for us to shoot an enormous amount of ammunition, which was delivered by the light railroad, by wagons, and by our untiring and heroic drivers. Whether "Fritz" received the full benefit of all these explosives is known only to himself and Jehovah, for it is certain nobody else had much idea where the old relics were dropping them. Occasionally he used to come back in great shape, and then there was a concerted rush for the tunnel under the track, with steel rails, corrugated iron, ties and bricks falling in a shower around you. As old Brady Ludgate remarked one day in his inimitable way, "I was running like the (untranslatable) but I thought I was standing still." "Say, Brady," said one unto, him, when he had reached, safety, "Do you think you'll ever go home?" "Not as a unit" replied that worthy with a grin.

The railroad track, the culvert and their associations were left behind on September 8th, and we went out for a rest and reorganization. The former meant the shining of brass and the polishing of leather, the visits of the mighty ones of the earth, who, wear red on their caps and gold braid on their sleeves and at the sight of whose splendor and magnificence lesser officers' hearts quake within them, and their knees do knock together for fear a buckle may be found dirty or a warrior not have shaven that day, as well as the digging of positions that we were destined not to occupy. Here our fate was made known to us, and we found that the flying column was to be our home

- hence we must adorn the wagons with paint of many colors to bewilder the planes of the wily Hun. Accordingly, under the direction of Corporal Pettitt, there was plenty of paint applied to the vehicles, as well as to the persons of the amateur camouflage artists. The result was dazzling indeed, for as Captain Donald put it in his rough Eastern style, "They loom up like a latrine in a fog."

By this time we were all "hard" and had forgotten that we ever belonged to a dry battery. Hence we started a canteen, mostly wet, and, Oh! Lizzie, you should have seen all those Presbyterians throng to the counter with their mess-tins. It was very convenient for Saddler Ross, and such as get "stewed" very easily, because they had not so far to get home afterwards.

Well, as I said before, the new lads arrived and some looked good to us and some looked pretty small and others rather young. Little "Tich," with his whiskey chuckle, often told us about how he would have been run in upon one occasion in old Lunnon, only the bobby ran right over him and didn't see him. One morning upon arising he donned his enormous boots and exclaimed, "Hi'm hall blinkin' boots and no legs." His song entitled "You're up in the world yer know" is a great hit, and nearly as popular as Stevens' masterpiece "Kafoosalum." When Pollard sings "Honey Wait For Me" and Stevens recites his effort, one fears for their future.

At any rate we received these strangers into our bosoms, and proceeded to relate all our blood-curdling adventures to their unbelieving cars. "You can't frighten me," said one bold youth, flourishing a large revolver, "for I want to go over the top, my brother is in the Royal Flying Corps, and I guess I can go over and get some souvenirs as well as anyone." However, this dashing spirit is now somewhat squelched, and about the only top he wants to navigate is the top bunk in the cold bleak billet. Another genius, with a scientific turn of mind, had a sure and certain cure for the plague that is ever with us, but at this date he "houses" as many of them as any of us. Astonishing how many qualified wig-waggers there were in this bunch, too. Some of them went down to Mont St. Eloi the first night and read Akety-Ak, etc., from the flares on the front line. Marvelous performance! Later on, another, with flags all over his arm, was requested to read the message being flashed from a lamp in a forward "pill-box." "Well," said he, after being wrapped in thought for some time, "If I had lots of time and it wasn't coming so fast, and there were not so many abbreviations to remember, I might catch a few words." Let us talk of something else.

One windy morning we broke camp and started on a trek to Belgium, that low-lying country which some of us knew only too well. After an uneventful trip we reached this health resort and were greeted with tales that made our blood run cold with terror. Our gallant S.M., after conversing with

The Battery on the March.

convivial spirits in the estaminets and Quarter-Master stores, (one can get tanked in either place) was particularly eloquent on the subject "The Battery we are to relieve," said he with ill-concealed delight, "has been wiped out three times up there. The drivers were all killed every time they went up the line, and new ones had to be sent up to bury them and take charge of their horses. Guns blown up every day. Only the S.M. and Farrier-Sergeant left to tell the horrible tale." Pleasant, was it not! Besides this, we were sure to be bombed every night and shelled every day at the lines, so it was no wonder we grew very homesick.

However, we finally got into action, and 'twas then that most of us found it in our hearts to bless old "Fritz" as we did the "pill-box glide" (to use Thomas' expression) or the "duck-walk wiggle" towards a concrete place of safety. There were five of us, one balmy afternoon, gathered together with "Stop! Flop! Listen! Safety First!" foremost in our minds, in the lee of a certain small refuge near the guns. "Old Vimy was a home to this," quoth Harry Chace, - whose memories of Vimy were rather vague. "If Vimy was a home, I don't want to start housekeeping in one like it" said Lorne Biggs, whose idea of home life was that of a haven of rest and peace and not a half-way house for Mars. There are going to be no culverts or railroad tracks or Dead Horse Corners near his little suburban bungalow. But the coolest man in the Battery was Jimmy Kingsburgh, who was getting ready for a trip to "O Pip" one dark night, when the spare parts were flying pretty adjacent and who kept wondering how many hard tack he needed for the morrow. Old Ben Case was of the opinion that he would be needing a wooden cross, but that was not worrying our Jimmy.

I guess the Royal Garrison Artillery have pleasant memories of our capable drivers and enjoyed having their "pawty" broken up and scattered all over the plank road. Wonder what the 'how' battery not far away said when their Isaac Cooke came to make out his ammunition reports. As old Jack Percival put it in his droll native style, "Those 43rd drivers would steal the beads off the Lord's moccasins." Andy Brown and old Dan Patch of the Kilties sub - by the way, is C Sub going to get their kilts in time for the spring push? - were particularly rude in pushing through the poor limers' plank-walk parades. Andy had a score to settle, so the story runs. Do not ask him about it, for he lapses into his native tongue when excited and you could not "compree" him at all.

Well the last day, as the guns were being brought out, all went well, despite the fact that "the blank-valk vas bombed to hell mit Gothas and mit 8-inch and the dressing station vas all blown up and twenty men napooed." Even Sergeant Tozer-better known as Towser, and created a Sergeant because he had once been a trumpeter in the Royal Field Artillery - even his gun was brought out, though old Brady had hard work to find it so far gone was it in the depths of the mire. Sergeant Simmonds is a man after our own hearts, though when he says that he jumped around a tree three times without touching the ground, when he thought he heard a whine in the nearby air, he is asking a lot of us if he expects us to believe him.

And now you all want to get a rest from this, and hear something else for a change. Great thing, Christmas, isn't it, when you can get a drink of rum without giving your age, date of enlistment, colour of eyes and so on before you can imbibe the life-giving fluid. Anyway, if you don't like this stuff, you can now wake up and carry on - as before.

PART III

Chapter III - 1

Holding The Ridge

There's a double culvert in front of Vimy Village, where the spur of the railway running to La Chaudiere forms a Y by branching out into the line to Vimy Station and another towards Avion. Just an ordinary railway culvert, but in our memories of the "colossal European conflict" it does not yield place to Mont St. Eloi Tower, the Virgin of Albert or other landmarks. Those dinky little French choo-choos will be shunting over that culvert now: there wasn't much traffic though, when we were knocking around there. Then the culvert was the last place on earth one would select to write a letter in, or sit around waiting for something to happen. Something would happen too. In fact, so, many things happened around the old culvert most fellows gave it a wide berth. There was no temptation to linger when one had occasion to double through it, for the shell-holes were too numerous and with that "just arrived" appearance that set one thinking. Many a time, just as you approached the culvert with noble intentions to go through in a blasé, nonchalant manner, the sudden rush of a shell, and black smoke drifting over your intended path made you pause and consider. Then, if you were the stuff heroes are made of, you probably made a dash for it before the next one, but if you were thinking of going on leave some day, you made a wary and lengthy detour via the Arras-Lens road. Truly, in that part of the country, the longest way round was the shortest way home, and, in thinking of the numerous times one has had to make those little decisions, we remember Stevens the G.S. driver's words in a similar dilemma.

It was the morning the Battery moved up into Vimy Village, after the 9th of April show, and Steve was driving the wheel team from the seat of the wagon, while John Derby piloted the leaders. As they drew near Petit Vimy corner - you remember how Fritz strafed it those days - the 5.9's were landing monotonously on the road in front of them. The wagon stopped.

"How about it, Steve?" quoth John. "We'll - er- wait a minute," said Steve, who had volunteered for the joy-ride. They waited a minute and then some more - still no let up in the shells falling at regular intervals. "How about it, Steve?" "We'll give him a couple more minutes to quit, John." But so far as they could see, Fritz was satisfied to pound the road all day, and the rations had to get up to the lads, so Steve settled his tin hat over his eyes - "Well, John, I'm prepared to meet my Maker - Let's go!"

Though the vicinity of the double culvert was rather unpopular, as we have already explained, still it was to be our home for a couple of months, and, in continuing the story of the Battery from the point at which the late Hugh Kay's history ends so abruptly, we commence at the time, early in July, 1917, when our guns were moved forward to the Y or culvert position. There had been few charms in the life back in Vimy Village, and the news of a change of scene was welcomed. That the new position was to be no more bomb-proof, however, was evident before we had got nicely started digging the gun-pits. These were aligned as close to the railway embankment as possible without being unable to clear the crest, while we set to work scooping out sleeping quarters in the side of the bank farthest from Fritz. Unfortunately the prominence of the culvert had made it the favourite registration point of the German batteries, and as any shots falling a little short were bound to descend in our midst, the interest imparted to living there is readily apparent

Certain optimists, when we first started excavating, argued hopefully that the slope of the embankment would be "dead" ground, and immune from intruding 5.9's. In a few minutes, Charles Ivan Junkin (he who after a rum issue could dissertate upon the merits of Falernian wines as set forth by Horace) was hastily hoofing it for the dressing station with a souvenir in his shoulder. He waited not to say "Goodbye" or shake hands with us. After that we had no more illusions as to where "Fritz" couldn't lob assorted High Explosive. We were firmly convinced, after a day or two of the exhilarating life there that Fritz could even curve 4.1's around corners. A soldier only ceased to be a rookie when he had realized, that there was only one thing they couldn't do to him in the army, and also, that there was no place from which Fritz couldn't shift him.

Speaking of shifting, can anyone tell us why the German artillerymen had such a passion for wrecking cook-houses or making more work for the Sanitary fatigue? Three spots in the Battery position were seldom overlooked by "Fritz" - and two of them were the cook-house and Isaac Cooke's tabernacle. So we dug away back into the bank, heaped tons of sandbags on top of the elephant iron and then started tunneling operations. It's a mighty lazy man who won't work like a beaver putting more earth between him and possible five by nines. Not that we had a great deal of faith in our homes' bomb-proof qualities even when completed, but there was always some one sufficiently cheerfull to say, "Well, she'll stop a sensitive fuse now." As a rule, when things got lively, we preferred not to wait in the dugout to see how much the roof would stop, but cleared out on the double for an old German tunnel under the embankment

Throughout that eventful summer, the 43rd appeared to be a "buckshee" outfit, for, after being disowned by the 10th Brigade, we were passed from hand to hand with confusing rapidity, finally coming under the wing of the 3rd Brigade, 4th Divisional Artillery. Though it was often a mystery to just what unit we belonged, there apparently was no doubt in the minds of the "Powers That Were" that the 43rd could not be spared from the line; so after other Brigades were withdrawn, we continued to hold the Ridge. Only at long intervals could a compassionate Paymaster be induced to visit our lines - these rare visits being followed by a brief rush upon the Canteen, and the simultaneous appearance of several Crown & Anchor boards, presided over by Messrs. Flesch, Brackett and Brown. For a night or two the lines re-echoed with such cryptic cries as these - "Come on, my lucky lads, slap her down thick and heavy." "The more you put down the more you pick up - if you're lucky!" "Who says a little more on the old Sergeant-Major?" "Nobody fancy the old mud-hook?" "Where you like and where you fancy!" "Well, up she comes - and the old man smiles again." While across the way Charlie Flesch reminds unlucky gamblers, "Didn't I told you? And you wouldn't belief me, you blanketty blankers!" Soon all the money in the Battery will be in the hands of a few, and time will hang heavily till the next pay day.

Despite our splendid isolation from the other Divisions, we were not forgotten when firing orders were distributed. Oh, no! The Third Brigade saw to that, and in addition to doing their bally wire-cutting and retaliation, Robinson's Heavy Group attached us and turned us loose upon Heinie's back areas. We had also a wireless outfit, the bane of a gunner's existence, and the unseasonable hours at which those intrepid airmen spotted targets was particularly irritating. As soon as we had slugged goodly piles of shells into the pits, we went to work and fired them all away.

It reminded us of the Belgian 75 Battery that was behind us at Shrapnel Corner when we were debutantes in the Ypres salient. When all was peaceful and calm save for the rumble of the transport wagons and odd rifle shots, suddenly the stillness of the night would be broken by the pandemonium of six 75's ripping off a sustained burst of gunfire. The infernal racket of the guns and the shells in their flight reverberating over Zillebeke Lake usually awakened us from only too short slumbers. "It's that cursed Belgian Battery," some one would exclaim wrathfully, but Weary Beatty would merely roll over in his bunk and say drowsily "Ye-ah, they've got another load of ammunition up!"

We beg the reader's pardon for this digression, and assure him we have only harked back to Ypres days in order to get Sam Price's goat, should he ever chance to read this. When Sam became too emphatic in his arguments, shortly after joining the Battery, some of the 307's would quietly drag in some experience of Ypres or the Somme, much to his discomfiture, so that at last Sam never ventured upon a sweeping assertion without qualifying it with "But of course, I wasn't at Ypres."

Every night growling Battery orderlies were sent over to Brigade to have the Battery watch synchronized - whatever that means - and then we had one of those two or three hundred round nightly shoots that Dugout Dick so delighted in. All this strafing was done with atrociously worn out weapons - not only was there little or no rifling left in their barrels, but they developed almost every balky trick of which an old gun can be capable. When the extractor of Don sub gun refused to "extract," one of the crew was stationed out in front with a handspike and ramming it down the muzzle, knocked out the rebellious cartridge case. The other crews were up against similar problems and with such an unique armament, there was some excuse for various officers' pitiful attempts to register the Battery. Occasionally a gun became so utterly hopeless that it was sent back to Ordnance to the undisguised relief of the crew, but usually Fitter Charlie Smith repaired the damages. A good fitter is a mixed blessing.

Nevertheless and notwithstanding, in the words of C.G. Thomas' song, we "banged away good and strong," and kept the drivers busy hawking tons of ammunition over from the Arras-Lens road, where the narrow-gauge railway conveniently dumped it. The old Fritzie wagon hauled half of Vimy Village over to the position for the construction of the Officers' Mess - Mess is good - and often dawn was breaking as the last pack tore around Petit Vimy corner bound for the wagon lines. One night, Assistant-Wheeler Foster- by the way, that's another thing that has always puzzled us, for who ever saw the wheeler who needed an assistant? - came up into the war zone and repaired a General Service wagon, which had broken down near the single culvert the night before. The boys had Wheeler-in-Chief Fox green with envy by spreading a report that Foster had been recommended for the Military Medal. On another occasion, when Fritz started raising Cain while the packs were up, Wheatley and Wood, two new drivers, look refuge under the culvert. They could scarcely have tarried in an unhealthier spot, but got away with it, so what's the odds? Some unscrupulous signallers tell a moving story of what befell Weary Beatty once in the shelter of the culvert. We refuse to believe this of Weary, and shall not pass the slander on. At that, most of the fellows who were up at the guns in Maroeuil one memorable night can scarcely afford to smile. Any desiring a fuller account of what transpired that night may send us a stamped envelope - it's worth three cents.

Now, anyone supposing that, while we were so generous in sending the Boches their iron rations, we escaped similar polite attentions would be very much mistaken. A particularly vile trick of the Hun gunners was wrecking the cookhouse about the time breakfast was up, and prolonging the festivities into the afternoon. During these frequent interruptions, we did not stick around looking for the Croix de Guerre or any other brand of cross, but adjourned to the tunnel till the dust settled down. Some charges going up in a blaze during one of these stormy occasions, "Chuck" Lawrence grabbed a couple of dixies of water abandoned in the cookhouse and threw them on the flames in the most matter-of-fact way. We mention this here as a bouquet for "Chuck," for we have a little brick to throw later on. "Chuck" may have been a little too conscientious about harness at the lines, but he was a prince at the guns, and that's where he spent most of the time anyway.

The imperturbable Jimmy Kingsburgh - of whom you will hear more later on - had everyone worried by his utter lack of respect for Fritz and all his works. The bump of a 5.9 a few yards away affected Jimmy as little as a "bump" of two shillings before the draw in his favourite pastime. The usual "morning hate" once found Jimmy engaged in wiping out his mess tin with the cotton wrapping from his latest parcel. While the rest of the troops sprinted from the scene in undignified haste, Jimmy calmly went on with his scouring, leisurely joining the refugees a little later. Perceiving that he'd taken the wrong mess tin with him, Jimmy dodged back through the flying dirt and corruption, and rescued the correct utensil. He rambled outside again before the shelling had stopped, and connected with a small fragment - a little reminder that there was a war on somewhere.

There is little space to describe in detail the events of those crowded months - the slugging of ammunition; the night firing; the voice of old McNamara with his "Any more for any more?" and the elaborate system of electric night lights, which the ration wagon usually put out of business. You will remember how we laid nearly a mile of narrow gauge, but never utilized it; how hard it appeared to be for the Major to register the guns, and how he usually decided to attempt that just when you had started to investigate some Maconachie à la MacNamara. Some too were fortunate enough to hear Dunc Irvine's comments after removing and replacing the camouflage umpteen times within an hour. Dunc never was in the habit of mincing words, and "Dugout Dicks" ears must have tingled where he sat wedged into the little O.P. on the bank.

When Dick waddled into the O.P. there was mighty little room left for the telephonist with him. He was of the Gothic type of architecture, with a streamline body supported by Baby Grand legs, and though one of those men "who are fat, sleek-headed men and such as sleep o'nights," he didn't allow us to develop the sleeping sickness more than one could notice. There was just enough room for a phonograph besides Dick in the officers' dugout. Nero fiddled while Rome burned, and when the 5.9s bounced off the railway bank and made the Battery position a glorious smudge of drifting fumes and descending dirt, the Major put on another record. From the safety of the tunnel, you might hear faint snatches of "Where did that one go to 'Erbert?" seemingly issuing from the heart of the bank, and punctuated by crashing crumps.

Don Ack MacArthur, who was a member of the "Brains of the Battery," once held us with his glittering eye and described the perils of O-Pipping. He had returned from a tour of the trenches with Lieutenant Graham, and was in a very nervous condition. It was D.A. MacArthur who spotted a Zeppelin one day from the O.P. in Vimy, and he was the only man on the Western front to see it, which makes the fact all the more commendable. In reference to a rumor then current that the 43rd was to be split up and a section sent to the Umpteenth Battery, Graham had told him that he knew the O.C. of the Battery in question, and he had never been known to smile in his life. "But" added Graham, "if I go there, he'll have nothing on me in the 'Gloomy Gus' stuff." But there were some of the Headquarters whose souls had not yet become as embittered as Don Ack's, and it was a joy to do a shift on guard in their dwelling, for they had usually a superfluity of parcels, and the latest literature, such as *Snappy Stories* and the *Literary Digest*. They read the former, and cleaned their mess tins with pages from the latter. While doing his shift, Jack McKen once became so engrossed in a magazine as to inadvertently stay two minutes and thirty-five seconds beyond his hour. Jack seldom made a mistake of that nature. There was no one who heard a shell coming sooner than Jack - he seemed to sense them intuitively and was flat on his face before others even heard the beggar. Some said that jack could hear the German gunners closing the breech, but that may be going a little too far.

Perkins of Don sub added to the horrors of war nightly wailings from his cornet, and when the quavering strains of "Alice, Where Art Thou?" floated out on the summer night, we wished he and his horn were with Alice, wherever she was, so long as it were far enough away. During his days as a gunner, "Perkie" had more than has share of close squeaks, and when finally a shell plopped under the wagon he was braking and deposited him some feet away in a shell hole, they made him trumpeter, and kept him at the W.L. The general opinion was that something was going to happen to him some day, if he stayed up with the "howatsers."

During the heavy scrapping in front of Arras that summer, with the British hammering at the Hindenburg line or Fritz counter-attacking, many furious bombardments started at unexpected hours of the night, which occasioned considerable speculation and excitement at the lines. Very late one night the startled sleepers at the wagon lines were roused by an excited voice calling "Get up! Get up! The Hindenburg Line's broken." The half-awake drivers had visions of a hasty trip to the guns, and what not but upon scrambling out into the moonlight, found Jack Percival swearing at the horses on C sub's picquet line, who had broken the rope. They had tangled themselves up hopelessly in their playful manner, and it is far from a one man job to fix a broken picquet line, with stubborn mokes swinging out in wide circles. The allusion, of course, was to C sub's Corporal, Jack Barnett, who was nicknamed Hindenburg from a supposed facial resemblance to the Prussian General; and other fairly obvious reasons. Percival was usually known as the Submarine Commander, because he drove the water-wagon mules. This was the only sense in which Jack could ever be termed "on the wagon," for his favourite beverage was not chlorinated water. He was also sometimes addressed as the "Limer," because, above all things, Jack hated a "Limer," and professed the utmost contempt for Imperials and all their ways. Jack groused more than anyone about inspections and harness cleaning, but invariably appeared as bright as a new dollar, almost rivaling a lieutenant in magnificence. Jack coined many peculiarly appropriate nicknames, and his sentiments were always uniquely and luridly expressed. It is a great pity that the choicest gems of his wit are not for publication - rather too forceful.

But it is high time we introduced to you, "Bert," our worthy Sergeant-Major as we have cause to refer to him frequently in the course of this story. We feel sure that he will pardon the liberty we have taken in speaking of him so, fam iliarly as "Bert," for we do not wish to leave the impression that we were accustomed during our long acquaintance to address him in that way. We realized dimly that such freedom would have been the height of lèse-majesté, but as we were formerly accustomed to call him by that name among ourselves, so we shall call him henceforth. When we forge to add "Sir," or stand in a sufficiently deferential attitude in listening to him, Bert often asked more in sorrow than anger "Don't you bloody well know I've got a rank?" Often we discussed the polish on our buttons or shoes, or the most effective way of grooming a moke, but Bert did all the talking, which made the conversation a little one-sided. He tried to make us good soldiers and often took the brush from a gunner's hands to demonstrate the ideal grooming process, beginning at the off-hind foot and working upwards with a rotary motion. We have waited alongside a notoriously bad-tempered moke, hoping Bert would groom it for us, but he seldom demonstrated on a mule. It always pleased him if, on such occasions, you showed no interest in proceedings, and leaned up against another horse till he got tired working for you. But we must pass on.

Wheeler Fox and Tex Snyder took a holiday in Aubigny without anyone's permission, and upon being restored to the Battery, Bert, much to his annoyance was obliged to escort the backsliders into the August presence of the O.C. Had the major been down at the lines, doubtless this would have been a labour of love for Bert, but piloting them through the war zone was quite another matter. However, as the shadows were lengthening beneath the Ridge, Bert hove in view with respirator in the alert position, and a brand new steel hat bouncing around his moist forehead. For once Bert had little to say to the curious gunners, who clustered around to view the novel spectacle of a sergeant major approaching the gun position. After a short interview with the "ould" man, the little procession departed, the air scout having some fun chasing Bert to cover several times by three toots of his whistle. Fortune favours the brave, and those of us who secretly wished that Fritz might speed Bert's parting strides were disappointed. The prisoners and escort right-turned and soon disappeared over the ridge.

At the wagon lines the lads had made themselves exceedingly comfortable in tarpaulins or corrugated iron lean-tos, but it was not until late in the summer that certain of the most confirmed bomb-proofers could be persuaded to stop sleeping in the deep tunnel. In fact they were only expelled by the Medical Officer ordering the entrances to be blocked up. It was quite a sight some bright moonlit evenings to watch the general exodus when Fritz threw a few odd souvenirs into the back areas. With the first detonation, scantily clad figures might be seen rushing madly for the tunnel, dragging blankets behind them, Fowke and "Aeroplane" Flint usually in the lead. Conditions there improved considerably after Dode Wilson's heart-to-heart talk with Bert during stables one day - unfortunately Dode drew him out of earshot, but it was plain that he was laying down the law to Bert in a manner far from acceptable to that worthy. Still this curtain lecture bore fruit, for he treated the drivers more like human beings afterwards, contenting himself with bullying the gunners, when they came down for a rest.

At the wagon lines Bert ruled supreme, and saw that the numbers one carried on with the harness cleaning. When not patrolling up and down behind the horse-lines, he could be found snooping around the billets with the perpetual query "What are you on?" But frequently the sun rose on a dejected reveille parade, which waited in vain for Bert's morning greeting. Then 'Dopey' Pettit stepped smartly forward and assuming the command listened without a mile to various No's 1 reporting "all correct," with only half a dozen of the faithful ranged beside them. These periodic retirements of Bert were attributed by him to *rheumatism* but some sceptics noted that his attacks of rheumatism (?) coincided with the arrival of another barrel of beer over at the 30th Battery. They professed to trace a connection between Bert's seances with old Jerry and his rheumatic cramps of the following morning. We cannot settle this matter, but only venture as our opinion-that any one colliding with Bert, while convalescing, would diagnose his malady as not rheumatic but aromatic - with virulent symptoms of a juxtaposition of S.R.D. (Service Rum, Diluted) and Beer. That dark brown taste was awful - now, wasn't it, Bert?

Remembering that we had once been nicknamed "The Presbyterian Battery," the reader may notice that little or nothing has been said of church services in these pages - and probably better so. Nevertheless on odd Sundays, the lads were paraded in bandoliers, spurs, and gas respirators to hear "a short talk." It is not for us to comment upon these "talks," or their effectiveness. A church parade entailed more shining of buttons and general polishing than any other parade; it was a succession of inspections and re-inspections, forming fours, and abrupt springings to attention. For, in order to appreciate the chaplain's message, the men must be drawn up just so, and every bit of their accoutrements agleam. With all this military ceremonial, it is not strange if to many there appeared to be an entire absence of religious atmosphere.

However, we shall describe only one church service, which was at once the shortest and most memorable of all. One bright Sunday morning, the "congregation" was drawn up in two ranks with several German balloons looking down upon the rows of buttons glittering in the sun, shining spurs and lustrous bandoliers. A more tempting target could scarcely be imagined. The chaplain had announced the hymn, and, led by the dauntless Bill Fletcher, the choir were singing bravely "Fight the good fight with all thy might," when a shell pitched over a little behind them. Everyone ducked and the chaplain bent down for his spectacles. A few trembling voices still quavered - "Cast care aside" - Zr-r-rp- a second toute-de-suite arrived with ominous roar, and without waiting for the benediction the congregation scattered for the nearest trench. Five-nines fell upon just and unjust and Fritz drew no distinctions between a church parade and a cook-house line-up, when either were unduly conspicuous.

Towards the end of the summer, the 8th Army Brigade was organized under Colonel Stewart, and the 43rd Battery was absorbed in the Flying Column as it was styled. We didn't exactly know what this "flying" stuff would be, but were convinced that any amount of flying would be soft compared with camping all summer on the zero line of all the German Batteries in the sector. Accordingly, one night early in September, after much heaving and straining upon drag ropes, we pulled our good old "smoothbores" out of the Y position, preparatory to joining the rest of the Brigade back at Le

Pendu. No signs of regret were heard when we turned our backs upon the ominous culvert, and railway bank. It was not a place where one ever felt exactly at home - the short distance between the guns and the bank seemed a "No-Man's-Land" - a space to be traversed quickly and with both ears pricked up listening for the toute-de-suite variety.

Chapter III - 2

Grooming Kits And Buckshee Pits!

We come now to some peaceful days in the seclusion of Le Pendu, a map location marked by two rival estaminets, halfway between Mont St. Eloi and Camblain L'Abbé. The life of ease was only marred by too frequent inspections and much polishing of buttons. We could sympathize with the infantry in the rest billets adjoining, in their painstaking forming of fours, but at least they had no horses to groom. The gun park soon presented a lively colour effect, as our amateur artists daubed the vehicles with futurist patterns in red, yellow, black and green paint. This was someone's idea of camouflage - to render them invisible to hostile aeroplanes - but at the same time the limber gunners were tearfully polishing the brass dust caps with emery paper till they glittered resplendently in the sun. If you would hear fearful and wonderful profanity, go to a limber gunner, who has diligently scoured his dozen dust caps prior to an inspection, and tell him the Colonel has just ordered them to be painted. It was this outpouring of mixed paints that earned for us in some quarters, the nickname of the "Camouflage outfit," or the "Comical Brigade."

About this time, someone over in Shorncliffe wished an extra section on us and a few buckshee officers. Some of the latter took far too personal an interest in the grooming right off the bat, and one of them, fresh from the Cadet school, gave an old "307" driver some inside information as to the F.A.T. way of rebuking a kicking "cheval." There's something about a balky, vicious steed that arouses unsuspected depths of anger in the most amiable of men, and to be rebuked for administering a few love taps to a horse that has just tried to kick you into the middle of next week is the last straw. Indeed, this broke old Bell's heart and thereafter, he sought oblivion in the company of the shoeing smiths, where he could use a sledge hammer on refractory mokes. The new recruits were, for the most part, rather diminutive, but they had the regulation sized appetites, and their propensity for "doubling up" and demanding "seconds" made them unpopular with old MacNamara, our superb hashslinger. "Short" McArthur, glancing over the line up of pygmies, expressed to the Sergeant-Major the desire to be made

O.C. of the "little fellows," while "Pee-Wee" Street, hitherto regarded as rather a small chap, at last found quite a few who had to look up to him, and went around with his chest stuck out. The cinema of the Y.M.C.A. in Villers-au-Bois competed with the various estaminets for the patronage of the troops, while the Fourth Divisional Concert Party over at the Chateau de la Haie played nightly before crowded audiences. There we had the pleasure of beholding Skeen, formerly with the Battery, before his warblings earned him a cushy job. Music hath charms, and for awhile, the war receded as we applauded what was really an artistic performance. But the hit of the night was unquestionably the "Girl" of the cast, who was a perfect thirty-six, and would have excited the envy of most of the queens of Piccadilly or the Boul. Mich.

Alas, it was soon apparent that even Bert's fertile brain could not find enough work for the gunners and headquarters, so the O.C. had the bright idea of letting the lads dig a Battery position lest they might get out of practice. A mile or so in front of Vimy Station, a spot was found where the digging was good in the stubborn chalk. By day, we picked and shovelled and filled infinite bags with chalk under a canopy of camouflage which caught the point of the pick at every blow. At night, the bags were shouldered away, and hidden carefully, and if there's one thing worse to carry than a sandbag full of oozy, gooey mud, it's one filled with wobbling, bruising chunks of hard chalk. One false step, and the business end of the bag fetches you a wallop that brings naughty words to your lips. Nevertheless, one of the pleasant memories of the war is a picture of Major Coghlan engaged with several batmen and lieutenants in putting a roof of I-beams on what was to have been the officers' mess. Also Chuck Lawrence opened his heart one night and dispensed a rum issue, and the picks flew a little faster afterwards.

Corporal Allies (what's in a name?) escorted the water cart up occasionally - very occasionally - a roving look in his eyes and a most palpable eagerness to empty the cart and get back to Le Pendu, while Jack Percival, the U-boat captain, called him names only a Spud Islander could invent and squirted tobacco juice over his off moke. The dirtiest night of the fall, Sergeant Tozer of the new section had his wagon stranded back in Vimy, and "Red" McDonald led a band of cursing gunners through the rain to lift it back on the road. Bert sent all the rookies above the height of four feet forward to help in the excavating. Some of them could not see the idea of keeping out of sight with German balloons looking down upon us or the odd "Fritz" overhead. "Lizzie" Hunt, upon being repeatedly requested to make himself less conspicuous in formed us scornfully "Hell! You fellows have the wind up!" But that was before "Lizzie" had seen what a 5.9 can do when it gets a chance.

From the lines strange tales reached us of war to the knife between Sergeant-Major Bert and "Bad Man" Mason. The latter positively refused to go up the line without a substantial shot of rum to steel his courage, while Bert naturally objected to any of the elixir of life leaving the sergeants' mess for foreign consumption. However, Mason won his point and finally Bert got rid of the rebel by sending him to join the chalk removers. There he installed himself as aeroplane guard, and might be heard at almost any hour of the day, cussing some rookie for giving away the position. Almost every night, bread, jam and milk disappeared from the cookhouse. If Ivan Junkin had been there at the time, we'd have suspected him of purloining the milk for he could get away with more of Nestle's Condensed at one drag than any chap we remember. When Charles Ivan picked up the tin, you could accurately call it "Vanishing Cream."

There we were startled one afternoon by the bark of an 18-pounder across the road and to our surprise saw a solitary field gun out in the open, blazing away in a little war of its own. This was Crowe's sniping gun, and we never found out what he sniped, but his little gun rambled all around the vicinity, making a most disconcerting row and drawing more attention our way than we were fussy about. If that was his idea of a good time, perhaps it was just as well he left the Battery when he did, or we too, might have been roaming the fields playing a lone hand.

Unfamiliar voices were heard cussing the mokes at night, and seeing little Tich clinging for dear life to one mule's neck and tearfully reviling the other, we began to fear the British Empire was getting pretty short in men. A driver on top of a team that are anxious to go in opposite directions is in a bad way. If he concentrates upon sticking to his saddle, the off moke canters

away, and if he persists in holding to the off moke, he gets yanked from the saddle. Only long streaks like Punk Cunningham could lock both spurs together beneath their mounts. This is a huge advantage.

The intended strafe in preparation for which we had built an ideal position never materialized. All that digging for nothing, but C'est la guerre. The lines meanwhile had moved to La Targette, and there we soldiered a while. Here there was a brief epidemic of promotions, and the Q.M. had to indent for more chevrons to adorn the numerous Acting Lance- Bombardiers.

For "one fleeting hour" C.W.P. Curzon was elevated to the rank of Sergeant, but before his letter informing Guelph of his rise in life had reached the base, Percy was a bombardier again. If we remember aright, it was C.W.P.C. who told Gordon Wilson in a confidential aside-"Us N.C.O's gotta stick together, Gord!" Well, only that some of us have pretty short memories and let bygones be bygones, it might have been a good idea at that. Brady Ludgate accepted his increased responsibility in his usual bored way. They stuck him in E sub to maintain discipline among numerous bantams. One morning the orderly sergeant stalked up to Brady and said "Bombardier Ludgate! Detail a working party for sanitary fatigue-at once!" Brady took a hand out of his pocket and looking over his collection of assorted recruits, enquired "What size do you want?" Then he added "Those look like two of mine over there, you can take them if you like."

About this stage in the Great War, *the troops had a bath!* Smile not, superior reader, for a bath was an unfrequent luxury in the army at the front. A ridge is taken here, a forest lost there, a few odd million of our allies are captured or an American soldier is seen out of Paris - all these epoch-making events make little or no impression upon our ignorant minds, but the long awaited announcement of a bath parade stirs us from our "fed-up"' apathy.

Now this is a subject upon which we hesitate to embark, and which we have sedulously avoided hitherto, but we believe that in what purports to be a history even distasteful facts should not be glossed over or concealed, and a sense of our obligation to posterity compels us to reluctantly admit that, at times, the troops were - well, like the proverbial pet coon! That such was the case has never appeared to us as ground for boasting - we are far from proud to acknowledge it, but occasionally such a state was inevitable. But just as there is hope for the warrior who, though he has been conducted to his bunk and his puttees unwound by tender hands, yet insists the following morning that he was absolutely *compos mentis*, and nothing to be expected from the would-be man-of -the-world, who raises Cain and acts the giddy goat under the hallucination that he's spifflicated after smelling the cork - so there is no disgrace in having "many in," provided you endeavour to keep the surplus population within reasonable bounds, but small sympathy should be extended to the chap who won't even trouble to go after 'em with a candle.

Now, fellows Who have made the acquaintance of the *pediculus candido tergo* inform us that, by carefully running over the seams with a lighted candle every night before retiring, the number may be reduced to a petty hundred or two, and those which are driven out of their trench systems into the open may be pursued till they experience the crack o' doom. Others tell us that concentrated creoline is very effective, but this must be applied judiciously, or, when with the shout "Battery Action!" you hastily pull on the saturated garments, in a little while you may be conscious of a slight burning sensation in some quarters. Then again, Sabadilla has its advocates, but here too, discretion, must be used or howls of agony will be wrung from your distraught breast. Passing over the common practice of wearing a cheese-cloth chemise, which affords better visibility, this is in our opinion the only satisfactory way to solve the problem.

After you have spread out your fragrant blankets, remove every stitch of clothing and rolling it into a neat bundle, fling it as far as possible into the night. You may be late at reveille, and have some trouble in locating your apparel, but for the nonce sleep will steal gently o'er you. So the reader will perhaps understand now, why after a month or so of these manoeuvres, and after he's worn his shirt inside-out one day and the right way the next, the gallant khaki hero yearns for the cooling streams of creolined water, and another change of 297th-hand unmentionables.

"There will be a bath parade for half the Battery at one o'clock." Well, let's go. But why one o'clock? Because it wouldn't do for the troops to enjoy themselves during the hours they should be earning their $1.10, and by leav-

A Night Attack.

ing right after dinner, some of them will be foolish enough to return in time for stables. Now, a bath-parade on the march is the sorriest sight on the Western Front and the despair of the officer in charge. For they look like the dickens; they march like rookies - and they act like lunatics. They have dirty towels tucked under their shoulder-straps, a bundle of disreputable buckshee clothes under their arms, and some have haversacks filled with imported laundry. Invariably, the bath-house is some ten kilos or more distant, and, when you arrive, there's an infantry brigade lined up outside waiting their turn, or else the blinkin' place is closed down. But we'll assume this is one of the times when things go off like clockwork, for a bath-house on a rainy day is a poor place to keep the reader waiting.

Very well. We file in, and the previous bathers are twisting on their puttees. They take a fiendish delight in telling us the water is like ice! A corporal appears and bids us make it snappy, so we proceed to disrobe. Oh, the shivery feeling as you tread gingerly across the cold mucky floor, eventually finding yourself with a hundred others trying to crowd under twenty sprays of near-hot water. But you cannot lose time for the feeble trickle will soon be cut off, you reach over the other fellows' shoulders and endeavour to catch the precious water in handfuls. The fellows under the showers are carolling blithely or yelling like hyenas, while those on the outer edge implore a chance at the water. All co-operate - "You soap my back an' I'll soap yours!" but just as you have your entire frame deeply lathered, something happens. The lukewarm stream suddenly turns icily cold - appeals to the knave in charge to "Have a heart, jock" are of no avail. The cleansing springs are shut off - and there you are in a cold, cold world with an inch-deep Pine Tar Soap lather from head to foot!

You dry yourself at last and proceed hopefully with your soiled linen to the wicket, where a South African medallist inventories your things, and hands out supposedly clean ones. If you slip him a franc, you may get a fatigue shirt, which some rookie rashly parted with on his first bath-parade. We should draw a veil over the next few minutes, but may as well give the whole sad story. The army issues wonderful, nay, fearful and wonderful raiment - you survey your shirt with awed admiration for the intricate organization which has made such things possible. Through a whim of one of its previous possessors, the sleeves have been ruthlessly cut off at the shoulders; of course there are no buttons. You scan the seams suspiciously, for you have long ago experienced the great disillusionment. Your undershirt is of the coarsest, most penitential type; the drawers - pardon our candour - are "shorts" of a cast-iron duck material, possibly formerly worn by a Highlander. One sock is a modest grey and extends knee-wards; the other of khaki hue barely reaches to your boot-top - both have been artistically

Mail-time Popularity.

darned.

"Tiny" Mackenzie is foaming at the mouth gazing bewilderedly upon a dinky, abbreviated little shirt, which he holds at arm's length in front of him. Even if he could get his arms into it, he wouldn't be able to tuck it under his slacks. Across the room the diminutive Lander is stumbling about, stubbing his toes in a veritable "nightie" - Tiny hails him joyfully and they exchange. So we could go on, for the infinite variety of the bath-house clothes rivals a departmental store jumble sale.

But at last we feel clean, and perhaps have a pair of home-knit sox, which we have long been burning to flaunt before the envious troops. It is one thing to pull "issue" sox on over muddy feet, but somehow one waited for a bath before donning those snowy white ones with the red and blue stripes. Which merely proves that even in the Great War, a little chivalry was still extant. Soon we are all set and straggle homewards, feeling infinitely refreshed and self-respecting.

That night you prepare to sleep, confident that you are free from annoyance for a few "What's that? It can't be! This is a clean shirtl Yet it feels like one; I wonder - yes, by gad, it is!, . . There, I got him! Well, blank these issue shirts!"

The October days went by in the same old routine of grooming, harness-cleaning or improving the stables. Very dull to read of, and even duller at the time. We had now been out of action for a considerable time, and all realized so carefree an existence could not continue indefinitely. The rest of the Canadians had left that area, and we knew it would be our turn any day to pull up stakes also. So the morning came when the 8th Brigade was summoned to join the rest of the Corps, and once more the teams were hooked into vehicles piled mountain high with kits; limber gunners tottered under bales of hay or bags of oats, while cooks grovelling under the wagons strapped on hastily rinsed dixies. Everyone remembers the chaos and confusion inevitable at such a time and how nakedly cheerless once comfortable shacks appeared after the tarpaulins had been pulled off, and tied to some wagon's footboard. Drivers are clanking around in rusty leg-irons resurrected for the move; gunners in full marching order are commandeered to load the cookhouse and Q.M. Stores' wagons, while the canteen proprietors, Messrs. Gourley and Don Ack McArthur, are besieged by lads sufficiently thoughtful to lay in a supply of cigarettes and biscuits for the trip. The drivers heap what they cannot stow in the baskets of the vehicles upon their off horses, in sloppy bulging packs, that will work loose in the course of a mile.

Fowke, O.C. feed-room, sitting upon a bale of hay, painfully doles out feeds and wonders how the Sam Hill he can get rid of the "reserve" of hay and oats he has withheld from importunate line orderlies during the past month. Above the confusion a clear note is heard, resonant and arresting like the noon whistle in a foundry. It is the voice of the genial Bert calling for some bloody gunners to do this, that and the other thing. At last, we are all in the gun park ready to move off - Scotty McLean astride some palsied sick-lines patient in the rear. The gun greasers have used all their straps and ropes in trying to bind everything to their vehicles, when batmen appear staggering under officers' prodigious kits. In vain they swear there's no room; there is no arguing with batmen, and who could understand Tom Hill's or "Minnie" Burns' language anyway? After the Major has decided whether chin straps shall be let down or not and Bert has fired some gunners' haversacks off the limbers, we move on out to the road in "column of route from the right, 'A' sub leading." It is strange now to look back to the numerous times we set out behind the gun, our worldly possessions on our backs, neither knowing nor caring where the night found us.

The afternoon brought us to Estree Cauchy, where we halted for the night, and the eggs and chips joints and estaminets profited considerably by our presence. After the horses had been groomed and pampered satisfactorily, we were free to seek diversion where we willed in the hamlet. Some, who in search of peace and quietness had repaired to the Y.M.C.A. hut, will remember the boisterous entrance, late in the evening, of the bantam quartette, Messrs. Pollard, Slaughter, Mason and Morton, who made a tremendous hit with melodies of supposedly Hawaiian origin. Soon we had to pick our way through the darkness to the hospitable cowshed, where we were permitted to sleep that night. Bunks in all stages of dilapidation awaited our tender forms, and what an impression that chicken wire made upon us through the thickness of one blanket. Peals of hiccoughing laughter and other hilarious symptoms presage the entrance of Don sub, gloriously pickled after deep potations of vin blanc et grenadine. One recently created Bombardier had unfortunately sallied out that evening in an immaculate new tunic, which he had been carefully preserving to wear on leave. The way home had evidently been full of pitfalls, for the tunic was hopelessly encrusted with mud, but the wearer was serenely oblivious of that at the time, and went on triumphantly reminding Frank Cunningham, "After all you're only my-hic-assistant, Punk!" At last Tom O'Neil in his quiet way put his exuberant crew to bed, and the sound as of many sawmills bespoke deep sleep. In the morning the suspicions of those who said the barn would be "crumby" were justified. It was.

The gunners pushed on in lorries to fix things for us, and the remainder of the trip was uneventful and comfortable in comparison with previous treks. Old MacNamara showed he was a real cook by handing out hot soup every night at eleven o'clock. It must be confessed that the ingredients were cheerfully pilfered from neighbouring gardens.

Arriving at Watou, a place not unfamiliar to some of us, we found that the gunners had put up bell tents in a muddy field on the outskirts of the town. We were not able to investigate them immediately, as upon dismounting, the order was issued to commence washing the harness. So, between one thing and another, the morale of the troops was pretty low that night, jammed like sardines into often floorless tents, discussing the crepe-hanging gossip, and cursing the German night bombers, which made the lighting of candles impossible. It is always particularly irritating to be strafed back in what should be a bomb-proof place, and Watou was far enough from the line to be considered boo-boo in the old days. Then, about ten o'clock, a big Canadian mail was distributed, and between letters and parcels everyone decided it was a bon war after all. Candles were produced and carefully shaded, so as not to attract Bert's attention, and the home news read. The letter you'd been waiting for made an awful lot of difference sometimes.

In a day or two, after the harness had been washed and burnished, it was considered safe to let us on the road without our disgracing the British Army, and we joined the stream of traffic that poured up and down the Poperinghe road. That night we slept in a field near Vlamertinghe, among some Second Division lines, which had been heavily bombed the previous night. There was unmistakable and grim evidence of the bombs' effectiveness, and this may account for the bloodcurdling letters some fellows wrote to their wives. Here is a sample from a shoeing-smith's effusion - "On the road to-day we passed twenty thousand French troops. A shrapnel shell exploded under my horse, but I wasn't hurt. In the field where we are sleeping nearly fifty men were killed last night. I watched them burying twenty horses that were killed also. But don't worry about me, dear, I'm alright." That sort of line is on a par with letters published in the papers, when the writer - probably back at the Base - apologizes for his writing, as a bullet has just blown the candle out. The beautiful part of those letters always came when the innocent recipients proudly published them in the local papers, and usually a copy reached the Battery sooner or later. Then the imaginative youth came in for considerable kidding. Passing over "Greaser" Mullins' lurid description of tanks roaring past him on the Somme, we consider that the wildest flight of fancy was reached in a letter written by Wheeler Fox shortly after the Battery arrived in England. In describing the passage of the Atlantic to some friend in Guelph - probably a minister - these amazing words were found; "Me and 'Buff' Robinson sings hymns every night up on deck." Imagine "Buff" singing hymns!

The advance-party had secured some tents from the Town Major, and we were glad enough to roll out the blankets and lay us down to sleep - perchance to dream! But we were not to dream for a little while. Soon the peculiar broken drone of the German bombing planes could be heard drawing nearer, flying low and in no hurry, as though deliberately picking out a target. Conversation flagged while each one wondered helplessly where Fritz would drop his tailboard. It's not a pleasant sensation listening to old Fritz overhead in the evening by the moonlight. You feel that he intends to select you out of the whole British Army for special notice, and the canvas of the tent doesn't look as though it would stop much. Crump! Crump! Crump! and they weren't a mile away either. The picquet lines alongside creaked as the horses plunged in fright, and the raiders had passed on. The next morning, the first gun crews went up the line and the 43rd Battery was in action at Kansas Cross in front of Passchendaele.

Chapter III - 3

Passchendaele

We shall not soon forget the morning of November 6th, when the Canadians took Passchendaele village, though it was not in most respects much wilder than any other day, indeed, less eventful for us than a good many. How still everything was in the early grey hour when the guard waked us to stand to; almost complete silence, but for an occasional lazy shell rumbling overhead from the heavies behind us. Here and there in the darkness, flashlights gleamed momentarily, as sleepy gunners checked the dial sight, while on the plank road, and over on the duckwalks silent files of infantry trudged past, with set expressionless faces. Even at that early hour, drivers were packing ammunition to the various Batteries, and back at the dressing station a long line of ambulances waited. These and other things one noted unconsciously in the hustle of preparing ammunition, and then the Major appeared, watch in hand. "One minute to go!" You remember the deafening din, as all the guns opened up simultaneously, the flashes lighting up the shell-hole pitted mud, and the air filled with the screaming of rushing shells. Up in front, hundreds of varicolored flares rose and fell in wide arcs as the frantic German S.O.S. signals went up.

Soon between the barking of the field guns and the deeper cough of the heavies, one could distinguish the shattering clang of exploding 5.9's, and geysers of mud, jutting up all over, showed that Fritz was coming back. As you laid the gun, you saw through the dial sight ammunition going up in flames, and writhing forms crawling away as German shells burst in batteries in front. After a while, the first handfuls of German prisoners dribble down the plank road, some sullen and dazed, others cheerful and pitifully eager to be friendly. Probably you envied them secretly, because for them at least, the war was over. Then the streams of walking wounded and the stretcher parties with their helpless burdens - the price of a few more acres of mud and stinking water. Gradually the bombardment slackens - " Stand down" - and leaning against the hot barrel, you light a "Ruby Queen." From gun to gun comes Major Coghlan, alias Dugout Dick, with a rum-jar under his left arm and a tin mug in his other hand. Whether you voted four No's last fall or not, when the Major handed you the cup, and said "Say when!" we don't believe you refused. The demon rum has no defenders now, but those mornings when you were wet and cold, with nerves strained almost to the snapping point as Thomas would say, "It touched the spot." Behind the Major came Charlie Smith, with sandwiches of bread and cold meat, which tasted mighty smooth.

Old MacNamara, whose pies had delighted us in Vimy, didn't stand the wet and cold long and went away a pretty sick man. We hope he made "Blighty" as he'd been talking of doing for so long. Certainly, we missed "Mac" and his tuneless songs, such as "Here it's always raining, Always bloody well raining, etc." Upon Macs departure, Slim Cottle, who had been wounded in the battle of Shorncliffe, was sent up to make our tea, but alas, Slim could seldom be found after eight o'clock in the morning. Poor Slim! He didn't have the wind up any more than a great many of us, only he believed in clearing out early and avoiding the rush. Indeed the only one we remember who seemed to enjoy life there was "Sunshine" of A sub. Sunshine, as his nickname implies, wore a continual smile, which Fritz could not remove by any strafings, and had besides a droll way of speaking of so many "cords" of ammunition, and other quaint oddities.

Three or four days was a long enough shift at the guns there - the dugouts were little protection against either the elements or shells. Digging down was impossible in that desolation of mud and a wall of sandbags a few feet square, with some sheets of corrugated iron for a roof, served as a place to sleep and eat in. You entered upon your hands and knees, and avoided straightening up for fear of lifting the slender roof off; probably, in crawling in, you upset charge-tins of left-over tea, which made little difference to the general dampness. At night you pulled a few sand-bags on over your boots, pillowed your head on your tin hat, and making sure that your respirator was within reach, went to sleep. A wash or shave was out of the question till you went down to the lines again. A description of the scene would be incomplete without a reference to the pillboxes. A pillbox was a bombproof shelter of re-enforced Portland cement, invariably filled with Imperial Officers or divisional signallers, and completely surrounded by water and the rest of us. Very few were so fortunate as to get inside one when Fritz started in to alter the contours of the landscape with High Explosive yet we usually fled to the nearest one, content to crouch against the wall, as though the mere contact with cement imparted security. C.G. Thomas, the gay Lothario of Beer sub, was known to have battered a passage into one once by bowling over an R.F.A. *Second Loot*, but Thomas wasn't worrying about so slight a thing as one "pip" at that moment. One morning Army Howard vanished from our midst, and for a long time, we saw him no more. The whistle of a descending shell woke him from complacent dreams of fair admirers in London, Paris and Sarnia. Telephone and all, he dived headlong into a shell-hole - needless to add - full of water. But Army always picked out a soft spot to fall on.

Seeing that we still kept puttering around Kansas Cross, one day Fritz decided to move us out with eleven inch stuff. The corrugated rattled when one of them landed even four or five hundred yards away. We didn't stay to argue the point, but retreated according to plan, and on returning an hour or so later, scarcely recognized the old spot. Fresh mammoth shell holes still reeked with acrid fumes, and of Beer sub's apartments, nary a trace. Blankets, warmers, everything napoo, but "Don sub" let us sleep in their summer kitchen that night. "A" sub's gun had evaporated, platform and all. Then somebody spotted it sixty yards away, nose in the mud, and trail in the air, looking for all the world like a crashed plane. Enter Leslie Ballantyne, puffing considerably from sprinting through the mud from Martha, our favorite pillbox. Major Coghlan here perpetrated the only joke we can remember him ever committing - "Bombardier Ballantyne?" "Here, sir!" "Have your gun in action within twenty minutes." "Yes, sir" - and a laugh went up when Bally finally saw the twisted wreck that had been the pride of "Shiny A." She'd been a good old gun, but as a quickfiring howitzer her usefulness was gone.

George Cooke was getting a lot of the lads away on leave - funny how when we were out of action or in a peaceful position there was no word of leave, but in the worst scrap of the war, with almost daily casualties, we were sending away eight or nine men a week; not that the departing warriors were loath to leave the war zone, but, with so many on leave or in hospital, an increased burden fell upon those who remained. Anyone looking forward to going on leave during those days understands the literal significance of the expression "Sweating on leave." Do you remember starting up the line of a morning, wondering what was in store for you, and meeting a couple of the boys riding towards Poperinghe en route for "Blighty"? In some mysterious way, they had wangled decent looking clothes from some quarter - not the quartermaster - why their boots were comparatively clean even, and they wore neither tin hat nor respirator. They'd a light in their eyes as of men reprieved from death, for they were going back to the world we'd almost forgotten, where folks wore pyjamas and carried umbrellas. So you wished them luck and sloofed along in the mud hoping your luck would hold out till that green warrant came through.

But, wasn't it some sensation the night Bert told you to get ready to proceed on leave? Why, you could almost have found it in your heart to like him at the moment. Don't you remember how every fellow in your subsection laid his wardrobe at your disposal so that you wouldn't disgrace the 43rd in the Strand Corner House or the Provence Bar? Then, after you'd borrowed Brady's tunic, "Red" MacKay's breeches, Jack McKen's puttees and "Mobile" McGhee's shoes, you went over to the Paymaster and demanded "the works," while the Medical Officer perjured himself by declaring you free from undesirable companions! Then you said "good-bye" to the lads, and undertook numerous commissions for them in London which you probably forgot all about.

As the leave train put mile after mile between you and the front, your spirits rose in proportion. A little m'selle waving her hand brought everyone to the window of the compartment, and you hoped possibly that all the girls in the Old Country weren't in munition plants. At Boulogne they marched you miles up a mountain for the night and down again in the morning to the boat. You really didn't feel sure of your leave till the old sidewheeler churned out of the harbour - though soon some looked as though they would not live to see England. Remember the hilarious run from Folkestone to London and how surprised you were that everyone still stopped to wave at the troop train? Then you were elbowing through the crowd at Victoria Station with a very definite objective - 7 Millbank. Perhaps we'd better leave you there - we don't wish to break up any existing diplomatic relations by exposing your doings in "the Smoke."

Different fellows spent their leaves in different ways. There were the sightseers, who made a sort of Cooks Tour of their fourteen days, and have seen all the famous old ruins in the United Kingdom, others preferred the old ruins who paraded Piccadilly, and not a few fled the temptations of London for Edinburgh or "Glesca." "Scotty" McLean was asked in Oban, what he'd done in the great war. "Och" said "Scotty", "I've stood whaur thousands fell!" but he didn't make it clear, whether he meant Ypres or the Strand. Even Jim McFaul admitted that it was more lonesome being good than broke, and was heard to remark deprecatingly, "They look tempting."

Later on in brighter days in Ohlain, we sat down one night in an estaminet beside Johnny Porteous, who had just returned from fourteen crowded days' leave in London. In an unusual burst of good fellowship, Johnny beckoned to Madame and asked us to name our poison. He drew forth a goodly roll of crackling new bills and paid Madame in a very lordly manner. She returned with his change in the usual dilapidated torn French notes, but these Johnny pushed aside as beneath his notice, informing us confidentially in his Alabama drawl, "Yuh know, I don't handle that stuff a-tall!" Over his beer, Johnny gave us a detailed description of how he had driven dull care away in the "Smoke." Producing his paybook from his tunic pocket, he showed us the entries which proved beyond a doubt that Driver John

Porteous, 307 something, had drawn fifty quid. We gasped in admiration but Johnny only commented, as he buttoned the pocket over the paybook again, "That's travellin' first class!" We gathered that he had not wasted his money upon the theatres or buying glad-rags. He had not toured the Tower, nor shivered in Madame Tussauds; for all he knew or cared, the "Maid of the Mountains" was cavorting around Westminster Abbey, but he spoke as a connoisseur about the various thirst-quenching emporiums. The final seal of approval was put upon an establishment when Johnny murmured reminiscently, "Good beer there, good beer!" Yes, Johnny and this man Omar Khayam had the same conception of what constituted "Paradise enow"- only Johnny wouldn't bother about the book of verses.

In contrast to Johnny's expensive lubricating, what do you think of Don Ack McArthur, who actually boasted that he'd only been detached from three pounds during his leave. Three pounds - with all London's facilities for getting rid of his roll? One could have a whale of a time in Mont St. Eloi on three pounds, but "Blighty" - " C'est magnifique mais ce n'est pas la guerre."

Oh, well, we've talked far too much of leave, - still it was about all there was to look forward to during those days, and possibly, it's a welcome break to the reader in the Passchendaele story. How short a time it seemed till you were in the tube bound for Victoria Station on your way back to the Battery! This time you knew what you were going back to, but at least you reflected there would be quite a pile of accumulated mail awaiting you, and possibly a parcel or two if the lads hadn't been afraid of the contents spoiling on you.

So we return then to the wild evening when, among other things, the major's dugout was hit, and Dick stopped a few of the spare parts. Those first on the scene say that Tom Hill was feverishly trying to crawl under a dixie, and Barnes fading out of sight towards the pillbox with a wash basin jammed down over his head in lieu of a steel helmet, which he didn't wait to locate. This he kept firmly clutched over him for the balance of the night, but let the chap who didn't have the wind up properly that night laugh first. There were a lot of dead bodies between the Battery and the dressing station, for the furious shelling had caught quite a bunch on the plank road. So as Red McDonald and Charlie Flesch assisted the Major to the Dressing Station, Charlie kept up a running fire of talk like this "Two shtiffs here, major. Three more over dere, major!" It has often been debated since, whether the major or the rum jars were first rescued from the dugout. The latter were certainly in evidence later.

Most of us had congregated in the telephone pit - muddying the inmates blankets and consuming their cigarettes. One seemed to feel safer jammed in with the bunch - did you ever feel, when you were off on your lonesome, that everything was coming straight for you, but if you were squeezed in with a bunch of the lads there was a less personal message in the whistle of a shell? It was not a particularly cheerful assembly till Charlie and "Red" entered with the salvaged S.R.D. Charlie wore a yard or so of bandage around his wrist under the illusion that he had been hit there. He said there was a hole drilled right through his arm, but he was not going down the line for a trifle like that. He would stay with the "batt-ree." While Charlie waxed eloquent, as he sat by the brazier, "Red" wore a look of supernatural solemnity, as befitted the senior N.C.O. present. At intervals the waterlogged blanket over the entrance was drawn aside as some returning fugitive crawled in to swell the company. Dick Wright frequently inserted his head to air his opinions up the *no-bonness* of the war, in that quarter of the front Later in the night Lieutenant Meldrum dropped in, having just returned from the O.P., and Charlie gave him a highly coloured account of the day's events. "Red" frequently interpolating when he thought Charlie was on thin ice, *Prenez-garde la, prenez-garde!* This caution was meant to be unintelligible to Meldrum, who, as we afterwards learned, spoke French fluently. With Dugout Dick a casualty and "Cap" Donald in charge of the 30th, who had lost their Major, the command of the Battery fell upon "Chuck" Lawrence", just back from leave. He appeared in a spotless new uniform, which was soon to lose its Bond Street magnificence.

We must now take you to the wagon lines, as you will be anxious to see what our old friends, Bert and Bubbs, are doing in the Great War. After a few days at the guns, you are quite willing to get down to the lines for a couple of days to dry your clothes and have a wash and shave. When the relief arrives, you won't tarry to show them where the charge tin of rum is hidden, nor the half-empty can of jam under the blankets. We step off smartly down the plank road and, clambering into a lorry at Spree Farm, subside upon a pile of empty cartridge tins. Jolting up and down, often landing suddenly upon the sharp edge of a 9.2 charge-tin - the brass hat in his limousine doesn't appreciate his ride half as much. The lorry threads its way through the traffic, the procession of packs, limbers, G.S. wagons, working parties staggering under trench mats or timber - in short the ceaseless stream of living targets that crowd the plank road. On either side, guns bark viciously almost in your ears, till we get back to the comparative quiet of Wieltje. So on through the ruins of St. Jean and Ypres, till we speed up down the tree-lined Poperinghe road, jumping out at Vlamertinghe to walk over to the lines.

Passing the gun park, we feel a vague sense of something being wrong, as though an essential feature had been removed. At length we realize that what we are missing is the familiar sight of limber gunners lavishly pouring oil upon the vehicles, but stranger still - in the stables mud-beplastered horses proclaim a lack of grooming, while no drivers are to be seen making the steel of their harness glitter with brasso and oily rags. This, of course, was before Major Reginald Armitage had come to make an efficient Battery of the 43rd. We have no doubt, but Ludendorf in his memoirs will attribute the defeat of the Germany army to the overwhelming dazzlingness of the British harness. Consequently it is inexplicable that when there was a real war on, as at Passchendaele, such vital factors as harness-cleaning and similar assininity should have been neglected. During those weeks at least, no drivers, see-sawing at traces with rags dipped in sand, sang that little refrain:-

We are the Ragtime Army-
We are the C.F.A.
We clean our ruddy harness
By night as well as day.
And when we get to Berlin
The Kaiser sure will say,
"Hoch! Hoch! Mein Gott!
What a ruddy fine lot
Are the boys of the C.F.A.

Separated from the stables by an ocean of mud lie half a dozen huts, which constituted "Home, Sweet Home." A solitary house on the corner of the road supplied eggs, chips and liquid refreshments to those who hadn't the energy to walk to Poperinghe for a real feed. We might refer, in passing, to the stormy pay-day evening, when Mason cleared this establishment out -

the Belgique proprietor narrowly escaping being crowned with one of his own beer bottles.

It was customary upon arrival at the lines to hit up the Q.M. for a rum issue, so, thither we go. Wading through the mud does not improve our already sufficiently dubious appearance. We fervently hope that there will only be Brimmy, or, at the worst, Bubbs to reckon with, but on shoving open the door we are confronted by Bert, our popular S.M. The personification of all the martial virtues, there stands Bert with stiffly waxed moustache and dinky cane, irreproachable from gleaming cap badge to topboots shining after Potton's loving applications of Cherry Blossom. What a world of contempt is in Bert's eagle eye, as he notes our unsoldierly appearance, and we are horribly conscious of our four days' beard and accumulated mud. We cannot summon the courage to mention a rum issue to this august personage - our only thought is to make as dignified an exit as possible. As a plausible excuse for our intrusion, we enquire timidly as to the possibility of obtaining a pair of riding breeches in the remote future. As mute testimony to our need of the aforesaid, we delicately draw Bert's attention to sundry gaping rents in the pair we are wearing. We confess that where we came from we "got the wind up" altogether too frequently and required no holes in our raiment to cause a draught. We also deprecate the intimate contact with the cold mud permitted by perforated nether garments. The argument becoming more heated brings Quarter Master Sergeant Bubbs, more generally known as "Alf," to the rescue from the inner sanctum, where Potton has been sewing more ribbons on the left breast of his tunic. Alf is one of these "strong silent men" you read of in current fiction. What he does say is painfully clear - he has no clothes, he cannot get them at Ordnance, nor from the Base, he doubts if they are to be found in England. However, he will have our name inscribed in his list of indents. Acting-Unconfirmed-Unpaid-Lance-Bombardier Brimson, who has been modestly hovering in the back ground, makes mysterious hieroglyphics in a book to that effect, first cross-examining us, as to the date we were last issued breeches. Apologizing profusely, we withdraw from their presence - with a last, lingering look at the 18-pounder fuse cap near the brown jug in the corner.

While at the lines, it behooves us to write the odd letter, so we drop into the Canteen in search of writing paper. Here Don Ack McArthur comes regretfully to the counter and surveying us mournfully over his glasses, bids us close the door. He can't tolerate a draught - it occasions those shooting pains and other maladies to which he is subject. He eases his heart of a long tale of woes and impresses upon us the hard life he leads in the Canteen service, the terrible responsibility, the long hours and the importunate gunners going up the line at miserably early hours, who pester him with demands for credit and cigarettes. Previously, we had always entertained a sneaking notion that the Canteen manager had rather a cushie job, but depart guiltily realizing what a picnic we have in comparison.

We enter our particular hut and heave tin hat and respirator into the corner. Little Tich and Scotty McLean are warming themselves by the stove, and welcome us - Tich offering to draw our rum issue, if we are teetotally inclined. Behold "Mobile" McGhee constructing a wonderful bed for himself and Thomas - an unmistakable sign of opulency in a hut where most of us slept upon the floor or that shelf contrivance along the south side of the hut. We could a tale unfold concerning Sam Price's troubled repose upon that shelf one night - 'tis passing sad that so many of our choicest anecdotes are "out of bounds" for polite ears.

To those who slept under its shadow the shelf often afforded an enviable invisibility in that sad hour known as "reveille." Brady Ludgate and George Magee (the "real" Magee - as we distinguished him from "mobile" or "remount" McGhee) were slumbering beneath the shelf on either side of a supporting post, past which Brady's long legs protruded, one on each side of the pillar. Shortly after reveille, Bert enters emphatically to eject those sleeping in without a valid excuse. As it is too dark to distinguish the faces of those lying in the gloom, Bert merely grabs the sleepers' legs in turn and demands "Who's this?" Shaking the foot sticking out on the eastern side of the post Bert enquires, "Who's that?" "Ludgate, sir, just came down from the guns." "Alright, Ludgate!" Passing to, the other side, he innocently seizes Ludgate's left foot - "Who's here?" "Brady, sir, going up to the guns!" "Alright, Brady!" and Bert passes on to the next sleeper, leaving a very relieved George Magee, who could not have given a definite excuse. Alas, it was not always so easy to outwit Bert, he had an uncanny habit of descending upon you, when you least wanted to converse with him.

There was telephonic connection between the guns and the wagon lines, and McAdam was given to diverting his fellow signallers by composing imaginary messages, which were typical of the usual tenor of the major's important communications. Hear Mac solemnly droning the following to an appreciative audience -"Take a message! Wizard, W.L.-acketty ack-Date - three bulls-send up immediately - one can buffer oil, tin Three Nuns tobacco for Major and relief for Sergeant Sills; break it, Wizard Forward." No comments are necessary.

Every gunner and signaller will gratefully remember the splendid hospitality of the drivers, during our flying visits to the horse-lines. It was something when you got down there to find that some one had kept track of your blankets and other belongings, which you had left in such careless confusion upon going up to the guns. How jake it was going through the ceremony of laying out blankets again that night and actually removing your boots when you turned in. For that night at least, you looked forward to a decent uninterrupted sleep, and you will remember how in the morning you slumbered blissfully till one of the drivers, returning from feeding his team, brought your breakfast to you. For life at the wagon-lines during those weeks was marked by an absence of fussy parades and similar irritating formalities. Necessary work was done and that was the end of it. It had penetrated the intelligence of those in authority that there was a war on a few kilos away. Even the omnipotent Bert went around a little less like Vesuvius in eruption, and reserved his maledictions for the Belgian beer.

The fellows were usually too tired in the evening to indulge in much fooling or amusements. Those who were not played out after a trip packing, or just down from the guns, were probably expecting to set off up the line early in the morning - so all were ready to turn in soon after supper. But a few by sputtering candles wrote letters, or crowding around the stove, discussed the possibility of the brigade being relieved, and debated whether we were really winning the war. Occasionally a little diversion was provided by the entrance of noisy revellers returning from Reninghelst or Poperinghe, and little Tich was nightly carried to his bunk paralysed save for his tongue. From that throne he entertained the hut with song and story, usually terminating with his favourite ditty, -

"We'll just 'ave one drink more
T' show there's no 'ard feelings,
We've been hat th' gyme before
Hencore! Hencore! Hencore!"

A snappy bunch reigned in the cookhouse - Allies, Ward, Cottle and Mason - and you will remember the long line-ups in the mud extending from the huts to the kitchen, when you occasionally raised yourself a little out of the goo by stepping on the treacherous surface of a submerged hardtack tin. Mind how the lads cussed Q.M. Bubbs when the skilly was particularly insipid - just like the old time funny pictures, "Bubs, he's always to blame!" Do you recall how Allies raved when you ventured to rinse out your mess tin in his sacred water cart? All he had to do in the great war was to ruin the taste of our drinking water, but it nearly broke his heart to see anyone wasting the precious liquid. But if you were to enquire for the real cook of the Battery, you would not find him at the wagon lines.

Up at Kansas Cross, the boys at last had a man who would serve up three meals a day, and ignored his own safety entirely to see that we had something to eat. We can but give a very inadequate picture of the difficulties under which he worked, his cookhouse a hole in the mud, two angle-irons for a fireplace and the rations often soaked through before they reached him. He usually had to carry over the water for the tea himself, and the dixie lids had to serve as frying pans. The smoke from the feeble fire frequently drew a few salvoes of 5.9's, which often filled the Maconochie with mud - but through thick and thin Joe Donaghy managed to have something for the hungry gunners. He didn't get relieved either as he should have been - no one was anxious to cook at the guns, however they might busy themselves in the kitchen at the lines - so Joe carried on uncomplainingly.

Somehow you seldom read of a cook being decorated or mentioned in despatches. There's no glory in bending over dixies or trying to coax wet fuel into flames with N.C.T. The cook is not an heroic figure, he's too besmudged from handling greasy pans and sooty dixies. So when they pass around the Croix du Guerre and Military Medal, they overlook the man who shared equal danger to feed the heroes. How often we returned to the position, after being shelled out, to see Joe laying out the jam and buttered hard tack, and hear his "Supper up!" His was a simple creed - to stick by his dixies, come what might, and have hot tea for the lads. And then - one day - when the shelling stopped, they found him beside the flimsy shelter he would not leave. A very brave man passed out that afternoon. Battery 'tion! Hats off to good old Joe!

As we have mentioned before, many, while at the lines, found time to slip down to Poperinghe - if lucky you caught a lorry and if not the walking was good. "Pop" had many attractions, and shops filled with dainty laces and all varieties of souvenirs reminded the more thoughtful to send something home for Xmas; others like ourselves, alas, were of baser metal and hunted high and low for the more satisfying eggs and chips. But, our tastes were not all as exclusive as Percy Cockwell's, the ambitious Kaiser of the Headquarters party. It is related of him, that once after the fair saleslady of a bookstore had painstakingly displayed all her wares, Pip Don enquired, "Haven't you got anything more expensive?" Possibly this was just swank for the benefit of some Imperial Officers also in the shop, for Percy liked putting up a big front. Remember his peg-top riding breeches and ox-blood leggings?

One of the typical nights there, black as ink, raining cats and dogs, while the wind threatened to lift the roofs, we met Mr. Ball tripping lightly through the mire. "Fine night" he said cheerily, rubbing his hands, "Great night, there won't be any bombers over in this weather!" For that was the paradoxical way most of us regarded the weather then. A rotten, dirty night meant "serene and calm repose" but a clear moonlit sky to us meant only one thing - the hum of Gotha's, sweeping of searchlights, barking of Archies and loud "Crumps." Rather provoking while you were painfully scrawling stuff worthy of a green envelope to be interrupted by cries of "Lights out! Blow out that candle, you epexegetic infinitive!"

Too soon the morning came round, when you had to go up the line again. Long before daylight, the picquet comes around waking the drivers who are going up packing and the reliefs for the guns. If you want to ride an off-horse as far as the dump, you will turn out and help one of the drivers saddle up. Undoubtably, this early rising paid, for our drivers usually had finished their trips before other outfits, and were luckier in the number of casualties. At that they had beaucoup four-leaved clovers under their saddles somewhere, as Jackie Saunders will testify. Not only did our drivers do their own work, but willingly helped the gunners on working parties, even "Pee Wee" Street wielding a shovel with the huskiest. Young Horn of a recent draft let his team get away from him on the Plank Road when a "Heinie" plane came overhead, and they say he spent the night in the deepest cellar in Ypres. The gunners used to marvel at Abraham Heights, how some drivers made their trips so quickly, until it leaked out that they were loading their packs from a Royal Field Artillery Battery's ammunition piles a little behind us. An R.F.A. gunner is even reported to have given one of our bantams a hand in getting the shells over his moke's back. But for real speed in packing, all will concede the laurels to Andrew Brown. Andrew went up the Plank Road about twenty knots an hour, hauling his team bodily after him. Rather an amusing side of the mornings ammunition slugging at the guns, would be the appearance among the disreputable looking drivers, of some chap just back from leave. His clothes were still fairly decent, and the impress of the Strand barber shops was still visible on his physog, but before he regains the lines, that will be remedied. All seemed to delight in kidding the chap who came back to that mess from the joys of leave, and someone would enquire innocently, "Whereabouts are you on the leave-list now!"- which was rather a heartless jest.

Some time after the actual infantry action, our guns were moved forward a few hundred yards to Abraham Heights, possibly to deceive us into thinking it had been a victory. It was neither better nor worse there than at Kansas Cross, only it took a little longer to get there, and the less of that Plank Road to be covered the better. "Chuck" Lawrence, Donnolly and Meldrum slugged ammunition like ordinary gunners, and worked like Trojans. The conscientious "Chuck" superintended the rescue of several half-drowned horses abandoned by the R.F.A. in shell holes. It was worth all the pulling and prying to get the shivering creatures out to the road, though one signalized its deliverance by a wild lurch that sent Dick Wright flying into the hole it had just vacated. However, C.G. Thomas didn't thank "Chuck" for entrusting him with the safe conduct of the salvaged horse to the lines. Like Most of us

Tom preferred giving the road a wide berth, and doing the "duck board glide." In palmier days out on rest though, Thomas took particular pride in grooming the "Pancake" as the animal was christened by Beer sub.

While a number of the troops were crouching in the shelter of a pillbox, during a little German hate-fest, Brady Ludgate entered in rather a hurry for him. Once inside, he placed his tin hat brim upwards on the driest mud in sight and sitting upon it, stretched out his long legs. "Say, Brady, what's all this talk about Land-girls and W.A.A.C's and Wrens?" Whereupon Brady elucidated his sentiments regarding the emancipation of women; from what he had seen on his recent leave all the girls in the country were in trousers or near approaches to masculine uniforms and he concluded with this gloomy prophesy -"They vote, they smoke, they've got our jobs and they wear our clothes, the next war'll be with the women, and it'll be a d——d sight worse than this one!" It is hard to say where the discussion would have ended, but someone in the doorway thought Fritz had cut the funny work, and suggested ambling back to the Battery. So in the cheerful realization that they would be compelled shortly to repair thither again, the troops quitted the pillbox.

All will remember that invariably in the construction of a gun-position, most of the material had to be obtained by illegitimate means, and the new position on Abraham Heights was no exception. Timber for gun platforms was pinched from the Plank Road or unguarded dumps, so that "Red" MacDonald was merely doing the conventional thing when he sent Chisholm over to a Royal Engineer dump to swipe a good sized stick for a trail-log. Curious to relate, for once, the officer in charge happened to be on the job and catching Chisholm red-handed, he strode up to "Red,"who was responsible for the theft. With an inscrutable "poker" face "Red" lent strained and respectful attention to the officer's tirade. What business had he sending his men to pillage R.E. Dumps; didn't he know better than to steal government property; did the bally Can-eyedians think they owned the world or what the — was the big idea anyway? He's a good mind to report him to the O.C.- in all his days he'd never seen such brazen, barefaced confounded impudence; what the —," here the apopleptic officer paused through lack of breath, and "Red" who had listened intently throughout shook his head sadly as he replied, "No, I haven't seen anything of a horse without a saddle!" The officer looked at him sharply for a moment and concluding there was no use talking to a man as deaf as that, went away muttering to himself about "those bloody Can-eyedians." We need scarcely add that "Red" was not deaf.

The 8th Brigade remained in action before Passchendaele three weeks after the Canadian Corps pulled out. We began to fear we were there for the duration. D.A. McArthur had a characteristically hopeful story that the

Canadians were coming back after a short rest and the most we could expect was a two weeks spell back in Watou. We figured that we'd seen about all we cared to see of that part of the country, and if some reader is disappointed in our eagerness to leave that pleasant scene, we can only remind him that we weren't "no thin red 'eroes" but everlastingly "fed-up" with the possible exception of Reggie Neelands and "Dope" Richardson, who were quite happy during those last days -absolutely so! But the rest of C sub must have been sick men for Reggie was continually entering the telephone-pit where the rum was kept, with a look of deepest anxiety and demanding a shot of the fiery liquid "for a sickman." A return trip was rendered plausible by leaving his steel helmet behind him and so on.

The Plank Road had fallen into a very perforated condition after the departure of the Canadian Engineers, so, the night the Brigade pulled their guns out, every available man was sent up in a working party to bridge over the shell-holes, that the guns might be withdrawn. The guns were lined up on the plank road, and the teams of the Brigade galloped away with the first gun they came to, regardless of what Battery it belonged to - very sensible stunt "Dutch" Jarmyn took a header into a shell-hole on the way out, but soon all were back at the horse-lines.

When the Battery began preparing for the march back to France, considerable of the harness was found to be missing. "Chuck" Lawrence would have got over this by having the lads go up the line again and salvage harness from the many dead horses to be found there This suggestion was not exactly hailed with tumultuous applause, and even Bert did not encourage this bright idea. So the 43rd left Flanders a second time.

Chapter III - 4

Jack-Pots And Rum-Issues!

From Abraham Heights and the Plank Road to the peaceful village of Ohlain was a welcome change. Beyond reach of the five by nines, where the night-bombers ceased from troubling, the troops proceeded to make the most of their spell out on "rest" while it should last. Back among the familiar slag-heaps and hospitable French folks - why it was almost like getting home again. In a day or two, one would not imagine the carefree nightly estaminet gatherings had a few days before been the sombre-faced men in the huts at Vlamertinghe. The war seemed very remote back there, the café au lait was excellent, and joy of joys - we were issued the bandoliers and other necessities we'd lost or ditched in Flanders.

Here we suffered a grievous bereavement in the temporary absence of Sergeant-Major Oliver (Meritorious Service Medal) who conveyed his vocabulary, cane and thirst to the Brigade Headquarters. Those of us who had Bert's welfare at heart devoutly hoped that he would get the post of Battery Sergeant-Major, loath though we were to lose his radiant personality. Nevertheless Bert's departure gave the ambitious "Numbers One" an opportunity of exercising their voice of command. "Chuck" Lawrence was still in supreme authority, and the way he kept Joe Cox and the other subalterns clicking their heels and saluting was a joy to behold. Oh, we were regimental those days. Take our morning parade for example. "Markers about turn! Six paces extend - quick march!" Perkins' chilled lips then blow the general fall-in and six subsections, buttons a-gleam, faces duly shaved and talcumed, stand "properly at ease everywhere" with bandoliers and spurs! Another tremolo solo from Perkins and the parade is summoned smartly to attention as "Chuck" appears from behind the stables. Section commanders followed by their respective "Numbers One" then inspect the rank and file. "Did you shave this morning?" "I lost my razor sir!" - "Where's your bandolier?" "Destroyed by shellfire, sir!" - "Have you no shoe polish?" "None in the canteen, sir!"- These and similar personal questions and untruthful answers are heard on every side. "Rear rank, one pace forward-quick march. 'A' sub, stand at-ease!" So the farce proceeds. The section commanders report "All correct" to the orderly officer, he in turn approaches"Chuck" and saluting in the prescribed manner says "Battery reported all correct sir!" Chuck acknowledges this soberly with a flop of his arm and draws nigh to make the morning speech. "There will be an inspection of the horses and harness Wednesday afternoon by the A.B.C. of the P.D.Q. The right section billet was in a deplorable condition this morning. The Numbers One will detail six gunners to remedy this immediately. Colonel Iwosh complains that three men failed to salute him while passing through the village yesterday. Unless there is a decided improvement in that respect, disciplinary action will be taken. Arrangements have been made for a bath parade, probably before the end of the month, about ten kilometres from Ohlain. A change of clothes will be issued to those who have any to turn in. 'Numbers one,' carry on with the harness cleaning." "Par-rade, dis-miss!" A sharp turn to the right, a snappy salute and the troops, ripping off their bandoliers, hunt for oily rags.

The tendency of drivers to remove their harness cleaning activities to the privacy of their billets was checkmated by the erection of harness rooms, while the gunners, under the supervision of two or three buckshee wheelers, built feed rooms and floored the stables. We weren't in Ohlain long enough to stop the holes in the walls of the billets, but no doubt, if there had been time, after improving the stables and draping camouflage to keep the north wind from the south end of the mokes, we might have fixed up nearly as comfortable quarters for the troops.

In Ohlain the recognized way of keeping warm in the evening was to sit in one of the estaminets till Madame bade you "Allez" at nine o'clock. The estaminets were usually designated by the name of the presiding deity. In the one nearest the right section billet a very comely damsel dispensed the vin-blanc and many bantams came in quest of her. Next door were two maidens of maturer charms; here you found most of A sub playing 500 and B sub hugging the stove, while Sunshine further endears himself in the hearts of all, by insisting that every one should dispose of as much café (?) as he does. Then there was the tavern up the road with the battered piano, where Yvonne of the Mona Lisa smile beguiled the lads into deep potations of very dubious Banjus. Many of us secretly marvelled how those Imperial Army Service Corps men could make a glass of bière last from six o'clock till nine. Perkins, after his lips were well moistened, would produce his bally cornet and fill the room with melodies ranging from "The End of a Perfect Day" to "Mademoiselle from Armentieres!" Many other quiet retreats there were, and each will remember his own favorite, but we cannot now - as then - do justice to them all.

The right section for some time lived in a barn as one large family till the aristocracy moved out and put up tarpaulins. They were kept awake at night by wordy duels between Pollard and Sunshine, or listening to Jim Rance and Reid trying to surpass each other in somewhat risqué stories. Who does not remember Reid's impersonation of the salesman with his universal panacea, lubricant and what-not-concluding with "and lastly ladies and gentleman, if mixed with water it makes a cooling, refreshing and invigorating summer drink!" One evening John "Bear" Wolfe and Thomas Vincent McCarthy staged a little sparring exhibition, but Tom was laughing too heartily at John Banfield's warlike pose to put up much of an argument. However, he finally threw Jack heavily upon Chas. McArthur's sleeping form, and hostilities ceased. The billet was tastefully and becomingly decorated - from one of the rafters hung a monument to the genius of one Johnny Walker, surmounted by the insignia of the Order of the Garter. Ivan Junkin had just returned from leave to Scotland.

Across from the cowshed inhabited by the left section, lived a good old dame who provided café and *pain et beurre* for the small sum of twenty-five centimes. There, one morning, we found Reggie Neelands sitting by the stove, busily sewing four wound stripes of exceptionally wide gold braid upon his sleeve, amid the worshipping admiration of Madame and M'selle - "Quatre fois blessé! La guerre pas bonne m'sieu!" But the yard or so of gold braid stood Reggie in good stead when he finally went to "Blighty" on leave. From London he wrote George Cooke to this effect -"By the time this reaches you, I'll be due at the Battery - but I will not be there!'" He was as good as his word, and herewith leaves this story.

We had a merry Xmas in Ohlain - very much so. The Battery dined en masse in one of the estaminets, our loving sergeants waiting upon the tables while madame and her fair daughters flew around keeping the glasses filled. Indeed, the dinner might be said to have commenced early in the morning with a liberal rum issue, which, supplemented elsewhere, had imbued a good many with a most touching affection for their fellow men. As the viands disappeared the gathering became more convivial. Saddler Ross mounted a table and announced his resolute purpose to win the Victoria Cross and complimented "Chuck" upon his successful manipulation of the Battery. "Dope" Richardson because obnoxious to "Mon" McLeod and a pitched battle ensued, but "Red" McDonald interfered in time to save "Dope," and led his erring lamb away. Bert and Alf nearly came to blows in a bitter altercation as to the position of Kansas Cross. As neither of them, to our knowledge, ever ventured nearer the front than Vlamertinghe, it is difficult to imagine how the debate was settled. Joe O'Connor insisted on shaking hands with everybody. "I know I'm only a rookie, but I want to tell you I'm proud to be in thish Baltterv." Gordon Furrow, being on the staff of the '"Globe" is of course beyond suspicion, but it was thought that he was he-hawing very immoderately for one so soon destined to be an officer and a gentleman.

A little jazz was to have been provided during the afternoon by select talent but it became increasingly evident as hours rolled by that the lads were getting more "jazz" over the bar in the corner. Jim McKenzie, almost in tears, sought "Chuck" Lawrence and implored him, "You're not a sparrow, Angelo, are you?" "No, Corporal, I'm not," Chuck answered, embarrassed a little by being drawn into the limelight. "Don't call me Corporal, I'm Jim" said the modest N.C.O. "There now, you fellows, I told you 'Chuck' wasn't a limer!" The kitchen door opened and Harry Chace, shoving his head in, demanded "Three cheers for Quartermaster Sergeant Ball!" They were given with a will, then Harry's head appeared again with a final benediction, "Blank old Bubbs!"

But the festal day drew to a close, and then half the Battery put the other half to bed. A terrible racket and cursing in three languages was heard in the sergeant's mess, where Charlie Flesch ran amuck. He stepped on the face of Mr. Ball who was sleeping the sleep of the sober and innocent. Who said that virtue was its own reward? Finally Charles and Bubbs endeavoured to mess each other up; we don't remember who emerged the victor and care less. So much for Xmas, 1917. We beg the reader's pardon for tantalizing him in these good dry days with memories of the nights he called "Encore, madame, toute de suite!" while fifty centimes remained in his pocket.

There is very little more to say about Ohlain. Mr. Ball left us to return to Canada and promised not to disillusion any friends who might enquire of us. We can truthfully say that the Battery was very sorry to lose him, and we were to miss him still more in the future. Perhaps we didn't always agree with him in the matter of a new pair of boots or another mess-tin, but what quartermaster could satisfy everybody, and we know Mr. Ball had an almost paternal interest in the boys. The Sergeant-Major, or any others who tried, could never get the fellows to address him as "Quartermaster Sergeant"- this was rather a sore point with Bert - for to us, from our first acquaintance in Guelph, he remained "Mr. Ball."

Speaking of Mr. Ball reminds us of rations and naturally with rations we associate the individuals who cooked and dished them out. Now Ward and Cottle weren't very popular as cooks; for one thing, they went around as black as negro minstrels at a Hard Times Ball, and besides they weren't delivering the goods. To make matters worse that water detail, Allies, had a finger in the soup. One afternoon, "Duke" Ryan (so called because, when be first came to France, he fastidiously spread a paper under his mess-tin, and actually employed a knife and fork in eating) was provoked into jumping on Allies and many dixies and pans were overturned before the belligerents were separated. We have always questioned the wisdom of the merciful chaps who interfered before Allies got what was coming to him. So there was a revolution in the cookhouse, and O.C. Smith was installed as generalissimo of the tummy robbers, a position which he only accepted upon "Chuck's" solemn assurance that he would not have to cook at the guns. It was pretty hard to put anything over "O.C." in the way of the odd crust. With deadly accuracy he could draw the line between what constituted two crusts and two rations. Nevertheless we didn't get very much to eat and welcomed being detailed to the Brigade guard at Vaudreuil. They lived high at Brigade H.Q. and probably even Jim McFaul and Warrener got enough to eat there. After Jim had unloaded his wagon at the Battery, his final question was for some hard tack, while Warrener held the inter-battery rice-pudding record. We didn't see much of Warrener then and seldom heard the familiar dialogue he rendered famous - "Cab, lady?" "Not this evening, thank you!" "Alright madame! Gedap - !!!"

So when umpteen brass hats had inspected the horses and found the harness sufficiently dazzling, the 43rd Battery said farewell to Marie or Yvonne and left in column of route from the right for La Targette.

Here we re-occupied the old lines we had quitted when leaving for Belgium the previous fall. In a short time a regular tin town arose, and, in order to present a better target to German bombers, it was decreed that the various shacks should be laid out in orderly lines. Building permits had to be secured from Acting Sergeant-Major Simmons, and, when you had a home nearly completed, some unscrupulous knaves would probably drag away most of the structure during the night for firewood. Meanwhile the fighting men had made themselves comfortable at Fosse 6, and, under the motherly care of Bill Howse, they waxed fat and reported a good war on up there. You could scarcely call Bill a good cook, his menu was not sufficiently varied. Bill turned out the same two concoctions every day, so, if you asked Anderson, the minister's son, "What's up for dinner, Andy?" he would reply scornfully, "Oh just 'This and That,'" meaning biscuit pudding and skilly. Still we noticed Andy never declined delicacies. "Gee, I'm hungry" he would remark soulfully as he extracted his fork from his putee, and wiped it carefully on his tunic, "What you can't harpoon with the fork you can drink." After these comments, Andy finishes the skilly to the last chunk of desiccated potato.

We have often wondered what lured Bill into the army, for he was not a pugnacious man, nor one to whom an adventuresome life seemed likely to appeal. On the contrary, Bill was a profound philosopher - he would let the fire go out while he harangued about social evils, astral bodies, emanations of electrons, psychic phenomena and what not. In his spare moments, when he was not cooking "This and That" or boiling the lads' shirts, Bill took great pains in the construction of a model aeroplane, designed to stand still in the air, due to "static pressure." Moreover, in his capacity as a naturalist, Bill flooded His Majestys mails with bulky parcels containing assorted shrubs and weeds which he shipped to England for minuter analysis.

At this position Jerry O'Reilly, the comely youth with the apologetic feet, won brief notoriety by nearly bumping C.P. Sills off. As Charles Perfection leaned across the trail to check the lay according to F.A.T., Jerry pulled the lanyard. That esteemed number one narrowly escaped absorbing the recoil, while Jerry murmured "Pardon me, kind sir!"

Bert MacKay, in an absent-minded moment, let his dugout up by the brick piles take fire and all his goods and chattels went up in smoke. We are reminded of another story in which Bert figured. The scene is laid in an old French-man's house in Hurionville, where Bert and some others were billetted during our rest there in February 1917. A box of excellent Canadian cigars lay upon the table one evening when the old Frenchman entered into a conversation with Bert. The latter, while not getting the drift of the old man's rapid fire delivery, was too polite a listener and at what he considered the proper points, assented "Oui, Oui." Thereupon monsieur would shove another cigar into his pocket, no doubt marvelling at Bert's generosity.

About this time, the hearts of all at the wagonlines were gladdened by the return of our old friend Bert, who found that discipline had become very slack in his absence. His first step towards reform was to ensure a larger attendance upon reveille parade. For the rest of our lives, some of us will occasionally wake with a start from peaceful slumbers, thinking we hear his "Out of it! Out of it!" or "What are you on?" Even the "unemployed men'" were forced to put in an appearance, and the indignation of Scotty MacLean, Tex Snyder and other worthies was beyond words. But Bert's pet aversion was the signallers' quarters. Entering these one morning shortly after the parade had broken off, his wrathful eye fell upon the inmates wrapt in dewy sleep. An awful moment's silence, while Bert gropes for words adequate to the occasion. Then whacking the corrugated sides of the shack and prodding the squirming blankets with his cane - "Blank bloody blank! You signallers living the lives of bloody gentlemen!" Oh, ye sad memories of the insolent trumpet that heralded another day of the great war in the harness room; when you felt for your breeches at the foot of your blankets and found the picquet had trod them into the cold mud; when upon locating the shirt, which for many reasons you had discarded upon retiring, you found half a tin of marmalade spilled on it - all the sad things that invariably happened when you'd deferred rising until the "five minutes" was blown. Or possibly you decided the reveille parade could get along without your presence, and, making yourself as inconspicuous as possible, prayed that Bert would omit investigating

LID GONE
EMPTY BEAN CAN REPLACES MESS TIN
CLASP KNIFE COMES INTO USE — TABLE KNIFE "NA POO"
SPOON AND FORK MISSING
FIRST WEEK
SECOND WEEK
THIRD WEEK
LEN' ME YOUR KNIFE A MINUTE, BILL?
!!!!
FOURTH WEEK
FRISE C.F.A.

your particular corner. He seldom did, and when, in the next hut, sounds of "Out of it" and copious profanity reached your ears, you either separated your shivering form from the blankets or suddenly developed some mysterious malady. This ensured at most only a brief respite before Charlie Flesch, or some equally insistent orderly N.C.O., rooted you out on sick parade.

Now, unless a man has to be carried hence in a stretcher, if he is sick, according to the characteristic intelligence of our army, he must rise, don bandolier and respirator and tramp a few kilometres to the Veterinary - I mean Medical Officer. Outside his sacred precincts shiver a line of the sick, the halt, the maimed and the lead-swingers. Here is a man with a bandaged heel, another with a racking cough, a third with hands to his solar plexus registering mortal agony and some who look radiantly healthy. No matter - they will all receive the same treatment. One cannot accuse the M.O. of partiality. He will give them all a little round pill and mark "M. and D." opposite their names in the sick report. It goes some what after this fashion. The Red Cross Corporal calls your name -"Here, sir" and you stagger forward with a few introductory groans, hoping you look the part. "Well, what's the matter with you, my man?" "Terrible pain in my side, sir, don't seem to enjoy my meals," (the latter at least is true). "H'm! Take his temperature, corporal!" The corporal shoves a little thermometer through your teeth - "Normal, sir!" In indignation, you assure the M.O. you had a horribly high temperature the night before. He doesn't seem to believe you. "Take off your tunic!" You do so. He puts something in his ear, the other end under your shoulder blade, and rams a spoon down your throat -"Say Ah!" - "Ah!" - "Louder." "A-a-ah!" "Stretch your hands above your head!" A wicked uppercut to your anatomy -"Does that hurt?" "No, sir!" - A left hook in the small of your back "Does that hurt?' "No, sir!" A stiff jolt in the ribs -"Does that hurt?" Doggone it! you don't know when he ought to hurt you, so, in despair you say "Yes!" "Ah! I thought so! Corporal, give this man a Number Nine and mark him 'Impetigo - with duty.' "

You're lucky when you go on sick parade if you don't find that the M.O. is not up, or else you have to wait until he's finished breakfast Possibly he's engrossed in a poker game and his batman bids you call in the afternoon. However that may be, after one visit, you will probably resolve henceforth to rise and hail the smiling morn before Bert's cane explores your blankets. Probably, to this day, through the desolate ruins of La Targette a wraith flits, at the hour of reveille, whispering with ghostly voice:-

"Me thought I heard a voice cry 'Sleep no more!'
Old Bert doth murder sleep; the innocent sleep!"

Fowke rejoined us from one of his periodic trips to hospital, and was appointed Past Grandmaster of the Feedroom, where he lorded it over the line orderlies to his heart's content. (We might explain that the line orderlies or day picquets, were those gentlemen who "followed the ponies" with a wheelbarrow!) Perkinchilli Spaghetti also wandered back wearing corporal's stripes and combined the duties of Sanitary Engineer and Aide-de-campe to O.C. Smith in the kitchen. A strange combination, if you ask us.

The arrival of some unsophisticated Fifth Division units in the area enabled our drivers to replenish their supply of nickelled bits and stirrup-irons, but furious was the indignation when the 30th purloined half their headstalls one dark night. By way of explanation, we should state here that the cheerful pinch-acquiring of government property belonging to another unit was regarded in the army as quite according to Hoyle. Absolutely honorable men, even erstwhile theologues, would not hesitate to appropriate under cover of darkness, tarpaulins or harness belonging to some other outfit. If the limber gunner is shy some equipment, he knows better than to indent for it through the quartermaster. That would mean a matter of months, so, he visits the next Battery's gun park and helps himself. This is known as salvaging. When your bedmate returned from a raid on another Battery's harness room, proudly exhibiting his loot, you applauded his "true Canadian spirit" and led him into the canteen to celebrate in a debauch of tasteless French chocolate or a tin of pineapple. But, in the dark moment when you felt in your puttee for the battered spoon, your only offensive cutlery weapon, and found it napoo - your heart was filled with righteous wrath, and you denounced the prevalence of dishonesty among the troops. For a meal or two you scanned suspiciously the dinner line-up for evidence of the missing implement, but it was difficult to prove your claim, as ten to one the initials on the handle weren't yours in the first place. Accordingly you did unto others as they did unto you, or went to Carrigan who always had a collection of salvaged cutlery in that mysterious leather haversack of his.

The winter was unusually mild and passed quickly enough. Baseball and football enthusiasts were soon looking for an acre or two of France that wasn't covered with barb-wire or chequered with trenches. By way of variety from the monotonous daily round of harness cleaning, a little farming was introduced, and a couple of plows abandoned in Neuville-St. Vaast were soon being dragged around by unwilling teams who resented this reversion to the peaceful arts. Ex-farmers and O.A.C. graduates shared the honor of this work, while "Paddy" Ruddy superintended the fertilizing thereof. The grain sown was potatoes, but we didn't stay around there long enough to have any *pommes de terre frites*. Someone else always gathered where we had strawed.

There was a fever of preparation for the expected German offensive and

many were the reserve gun-pits we dug between Thelus and Neuville-St.Vaast. As these were invariably situated in the most inaccessible positions, among old craters and half-filled trenches, they could probably never have been utilized, had it been necessary to retire - but these working parties at least enabled the latest recruits to get within view of the war. Possibly, too, the morale of the troops was improved by knowing where they were to beat it when Fritz came over. We were further encouraged by eloquent extracts from Army Orders wherein General Sir Arthur Currie exhorted us to fight to the last man, and assured us our names would go down in a big splash of glory to future generations; all of which was very comforting and - yet - well, some of us weren't awfully keen on posthumous honors. "Dope" Richardson, after a bored perusal of the aforesaid "Orders," voiced the sentiments of the majority when he said, "Apres la guerre, I'd a d—— sight sooner have people say of me 'Here he comes' than 'There he *lies!*'" We propose taking the reader around the various quarters at the lines to see the inmates during a typical evening. There is a strange assortment in one of the big Nissen huts and we might look in on them first. The soloist by the stove with the face of a movie idol is "Push" Pulling, who is singing the sad adventures of one Nellie, and the man "who done her wrong." "Red" Finney is regretfully narrating to a sympathetic audience how the "bones" failed to speak to him or why he told Bert off at stables. George Sharp, Mike Gleason, Wilson and Carrigan are engaged in a quiet game of 500. Quiet until Carrie accuses Wilson of renigging. "Sunshine" is trying to sleep in his bed, hauled with much puffing from abandoned lines some kilos distant. He has half the firewood of the hut ranged within reach of his hand to drive off practical jokers. Bell, he of the Napoleonic attitude, one hand to his breast! - is unconscious upon the floor. He went to Mont St. Eloi as horseholder for someone going on leave! The boys took the legs of his bunk for fuel, but the "bombardier" never troubled to replace them.

A little argument with the door and Johnny Porteous enters after a solitary reunion with Messrs. Bass and Guiness in some foreign canteen. Johnny is moved to, song. "Steamboat Bill, Alabama Bound, Three loud cheers and away she goes! Whoo! Whoo! Whoo-E!" "Where've you been, you old sinner?" "Way down at the D.A.C. Good beer there, good beer." Nevertheless Johnny will be washed, shaved and buttons polished before the rest reluctantly "show a leg" in the morning.

From across the way, above the plinking of a mandolin, come Pollard's liquid notes in a falsetto version- or rather perversion - of "Il Trovatore." But keep away from the bantams! If lured by the siren's voices you step inside, Mason immediately suggests a little of the national pastime. After being reduced to selling a green envelope for a franc to stay in the last pot, you will depart poorer and wiser, and someone in Canada will receive but the "I'm well and hope you are too," which is all you're willing to have scrutinized by the "O.C. wagon lines."

Raised voices with broad Scotch accents lead us to the shack where "Watty" Walker is stirring an infantry mess-tin full of Quaker Oats mush, his face alight with anticipation. "Mon" McLeod hails us with "Hae ye got a seegar-rette, mon?" "No, but here's some Flags!" Great bunch, the porridge-eaters. The kindest comment O.C. Smith ever heard upon his cooking was from "Watty" Walker, as he returned for a second or third issue of porridge at breakfast" "Yon's the stuff tae gie the troops!"

Did space permit, we could visit Beer sub's tarp and see "Biscuitface" MacKay devouring Huntley and Palmers wafers, a package at a time, or Rudy Corbett winning somebody's money, Sam Price anointing his remaining hairs with the Seven Sutherland Sisters, or Ivan Junkin reading F.A.T. and the 4.5 Q.F. Howitzer Manual. We would take you into the Canteen to watch the run on brasso and emery paper for the morrow's inspection and "Dope" Richardson drinking all by himself at the far end of the counter. We could call on the employed men, who are probably making souvenirs of shellcases, etc., they had time for such things - but a complete tour of inspection is impossible, and one "bivvy" is much like another.

Thomas Vincent McCarthy had found his way back to his old love Busy B. but being C.C.R.C. was not actually on the strength. After an uneasy sojourn, T.V. reverted to the B.A.C. which Lieutenant Matthews, who much

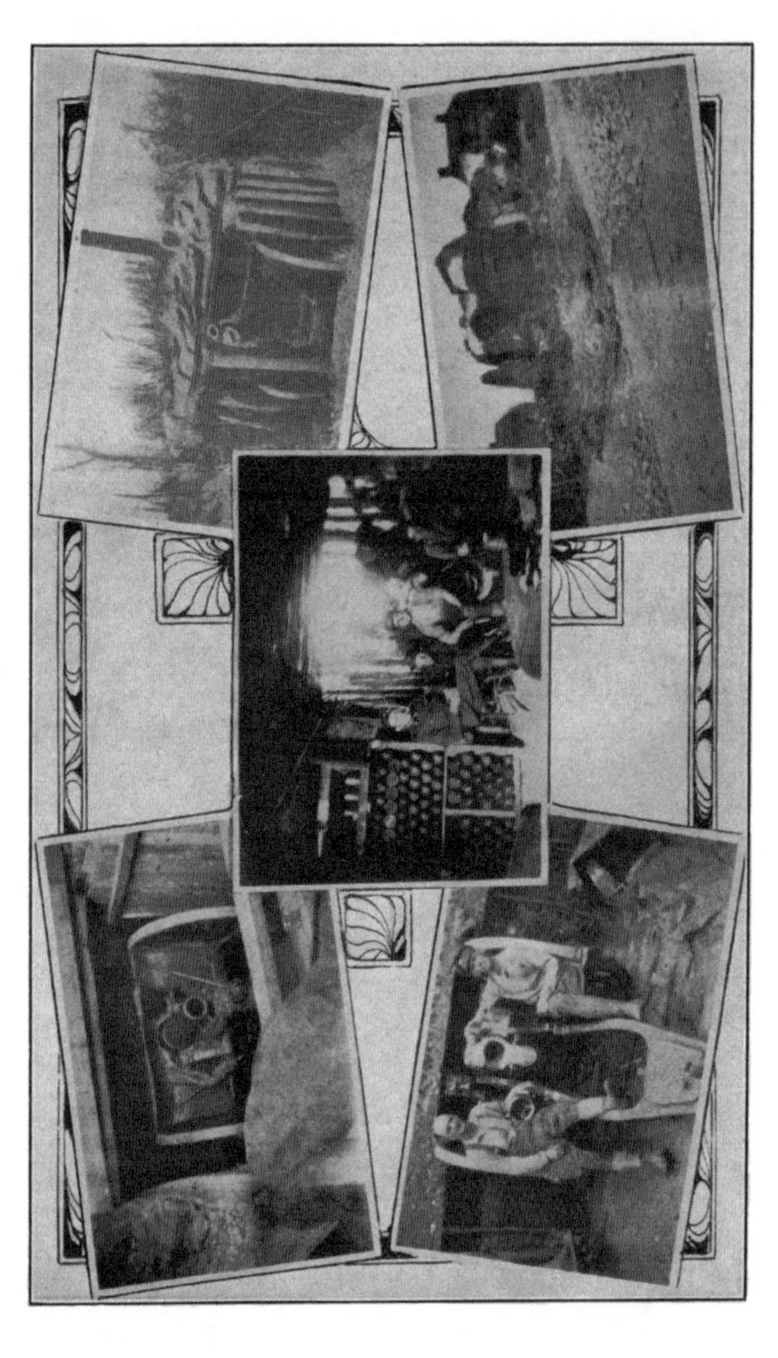

Gun-pit Glimpses.

to his disgust had wound up there, feelingly described as follows -"The 8th Brigade" he confided to, Joe Cox, "is the —— of the Canadian Corps, but the B.A.C. is the - —- of the Brigade, *and I'm the* —- of the B.A.C.!" So of an evening, Tom McCarthy and Sammy Murphy shook the mud of the B.A.C. lines from their feet and came over to the 43rd, where Murphy was joyfully haled into Shiny A and Tom slid into B sub tarp. When in good form Tom's dissertations were only excelled by Sam's impromptu poetry and repartee. As Sam's effervescent spirits were infectious, their visits are a joy to remember and it was late ere the exiles sought each other for mutual support upon the homeward trail.

As Johnny Porteous left us shortly for Brigade Headquarters, and from there to England - via the Colonel's horse registering on his jaw, before he leaves these pages we wish to produce a final proof of his iron constitution. Carrigan, a very ascetic youth, was wont to receive bottles of concentrated raspberry vinegar from Toronto. One night, while Carrie slept, the bottle and a box of shredded wheat lay by his bed. Johnny came in late, oh very late, and saw the biscuits. "Mat yuh got here, you skinny blank?" he asked, stuffing a dry biscuit into his mouth, for Johnny, though not a Bolshevik, believed in the equal distribution of property. The cereal proving very dry eating, Johnny voiced his disapproval of the same, and looked around eagerly for something wet to aid in the process of mastication. The ruby-red raspberry vinegar looked hopeful, and Johnny finished it at a gulp without making a face. Those who expected sudden results were disappointed, he merely remarked as he appropriated Dick Diamond's candle that "the dope had some kick to it." This was also his only comment as he spat out teeth and tobacco when the Colonel's horse kicked him.

From the guns came glowing accounts of wild joy-riding on the narrow gauge, C.G. Thomas and Brady Ludgate having an opportunity to show their railroading skill. Rudy Corbett assaying to coast down grade was unable to check the car's flight, and let it get away from him. It shot away with rapidly accelerating speed, till it left the track in the valley below. For this exploit Rudy was summoned to an interview with the O.C. to be congratulated in person.

General Currie honored the lads by a visit and had a little palaver with "Push" Pulling, the Adonis of A sub. "And where do you come from?" his nibs enquired in that "young-feller-me-lad" tone, considered appropriate by officers in addressing the nonentities in the ranks. "From Windsor, sir." Sir Arthur was in a reminiscent mood, - "Windsor! Oh, yes! Do you remember how you rushed across the ferry with a nickel in your hand for the fare-box, but you never dropped it in?" Push remembered. "Why," continued the august one, "I stopped in Windsor over night once, the year all the bed-bugs in North America attended a convention there!" We are sorry we cannot remember any nobler sentiments of Sir Arthur's, but this story is shy of lofty sentiments any way. George Edward Cooke turned one of Sir Arthur's own orders against him by refusing to sell Mr. Bass's Ale to the General and his staff out of hours. But after braving the dangers of the front on a peaceful day to pay us a call, George shouldn't have sent them away thirsty. As the General, followed by his attendant "brass-hats" took his departure, Simpson, we are ashamed to record, called after him, - "Have an apple, Arthur, have an apple!" Now, there wasn't an apple within many parasangs of Fosse 6, but we believe that the report of that friendly offering was responsible for the article in the "Canadian Record" in which the writer (also a General) referred to Sir Arthur as "idolized by all the men of the Corps."

But swift retribution overtook Simmy not long afterwards. After a nights shoot when the other gunners went back to sleep, Simmy, as gun greaser, remained to straighten up the pit and clean the gun for the morning inspection. Faithfully and well he labored and the appearance of Shiny A was warmly praised by the O.C. With light heart, Simmy prepared for a well-earned rest, intending to sleep till after dinner at least,-

For he while his companions slept
Had scoured the breech-block through the night!

On his way to his dugout he was nabbed by an ungrateful Lieutenant Matthews and sent away with a working party. Such are the tragedies of war.

It must be kept in mind that during this time, the so widely advertised German offensive, was expected daily. One night, Joe Cox with a telephonist was in a deep dugout at Battalion H.Q., when a little trench mortar strafe started. It sounded to Joe like the Big German Push, the Day of judgment and a Lake Huron thunderstorm rolled into one. To the amusement of an infantry officer present, reaching for his tin hat, he called excitedly to the telephonist "Get ready to run, get ready to run!" When Dunc Irvine heard of this, he shifted his old pipe a little and said drily, "Well, all of us won't run." No, old Dunc wasn't the running kind, you don't find them more chuck-full of sand right through than Dunc Irvine - "and so say all of us!"

Meanwhile "Chuck" Lawrence went to Brigade H.Q. as acting Adjutant, and three or four new officers came in his place. First there was Major Reginald S. Armitage, who had formerly been with the Fifth Division, and allowance must be made for that, when we refer to his passion for shining steel and well-groomed mokes. Next in order of rank came Captain Craig, soon dubbed the "Red Hussar" from his auburn locks and an unpopular brand of "Issue" cigarettes. Let us not forget also, Leslie Wright, a captivating youth who seemed too good to be true. The batmen reported that Leslie looked not upon the "Scotch" when it fizzed, but if he didn't get the value of his mess-dues in the joy-water, he evened up by devouring all the eats in sight. His favorite confection was "Chocolat-du Menier" and often on the march we envied his fiery steed, as Leslie crammed bars of chocolate down the critter's mouth. Last, but not least, "Sid" Williams, who was a pretty good scout. Having introduced these arrivals, we continue our revelations.

Well, you remember how Fritz showed his hand at last; how each day the line of captive ballons south of Arras moved perceptibly westwards; the contradictory rumours and frequent stand-to's. However, our immediate front was not threatened and beyond the back areas receiving some annoying attentions, we were not visibly affected. It became rather a nuisance though taking the horses off the lines and it was a bore building sand-bag walls around the tarpaulins. It was even more disconcerting when Fritz threw the odd round into the vicinity at night, and Tex Snyder and his colleagues took to digging down - way down. After a protracted strafe wherein Fritz lavishly peppered the countryside, some disgusted "fed-up" would remark - "and they say Fritz is out of ammunition." (See daily papers of that date.)

One afternoon just as the parade fell in, a "dud" plopped into the pile of fertilizer between us and the 30th stables. Scarcely had everyone straightened up after ducking for that one, when - zip - most of the cookhouse was in the air. The staff of chefs emerged in a hurry, fortunately no one was hit though how O.C. and Tony escaped is a mystery. A case of bully-beef blown heavenwards nearly beaned Dick Diamond as he crouched under the water-cart. Tony was a trifle shaken up and a little bruised from odd chunks of the cookhouse landing on him and, as they led him towards the Dressing Station, declared emphatically "No more da cookahousa for me!"

All Batteries were issued two Lewis guns, mainly for anti-aircraft work, and some gunners took a course down in Houdain, where they were taught the young idea to shoot! Jerry O'Reilly was very keen and became the terror of all the British planes in the neighbourhood. One morning Jerry decided it was high time to clean the gun so that Bert would think there was some work attached to being a Lewis-gunner. Pointing the gun skywards he cut loose with a nice little burst to loosen up the rust and one of our intrepid airmen, peacefully patrolling the Arras-Lens road, took a couple of bullets in his arm. Jerry was awfully put out when he heard of this. If he could have got near the wounded aviator, he would doubtless have said "Pardon me, kind sir!" Still, Jerry meant well and we know of nothing further against him, except that he came from Oakville.

Now, every officer in the Great War had not only a groom at his beck and call, but a *valet de chambre,* and the Red Hussar was soon seeking a batman to keep him dressed in a manner befitting his three stars. It had always been hard to find material for officers' servants in the 43rd Battery, and none appeared to be tumbling over themselves demanding the privilege of "brasso-izing" the Captain's buttons or saddle-soaping his Sam Browne. So when no voluntary applicants for the position came forward, the Red Hussar sought old Bert and requested him to make the necessary overtures to some likely gunner or driver. When Bert enquired that night of the various sergeants whether they had any one qualified for such a task, "Lou" McMillan, in order to have a joke on a Spud Island compatriot, soberly suggested Jack Percival. Accordingly, at stables Bert stalked over to Jack as he groomed his team to the accompaniment of unique Spud Island profanity. "Driver Percival!" quoth Bert "I've got a bloody good job for you." "What is it?" Jack enquired expectantly, yet suspiciously withal - for he was a sufficiently "old soldier" to doubt the possibility of any good thing coming from the sergeant-major. "Captain Craig," answered Bert, "is looking for a batman, and I told him you were the very man." . . . . The grooming brush fell unnoticed as Jack contemptuously thrust his hand, palm down, towards the ground in a significant gesture. "Go way!" he spluttered, "go way for —- sake! What do you take me for? I'm not a lime-juicer, I'm a Canadian! Get one of your limers to shine his shoes!" After this explosion, Jack returned to his team and Bert walked away without a word. Those who knew Jack Percival will be able to imagine the disgusted look upon his face upon being proferred the duties of a batman - fed-up was Jack to a degree, though his buttons dazzled the eye, and he'd his own ideas concerning our vaunted democracy.

So March passed, a month of discouraging reports, but we weren't drawn into the fracas and slept fairly soundly withal. For the possibility of being aroused by the German army had small terrors for those who were hardened to being prodded into wakefulness by Bert's cane. The "Red Hussar" had quite a detective instinct and "Hawkshawed" around the billets in the manner of the silently stalking sleuth. Personally we preferred Bert's methods. They were at least painfully direct. "Red" however was at a disadvantage in not knowing us personally and could be bluffed, but good old Bert! - alas, he knew our uprisings and downsittings far too well.

About the time the Fifth Army and the Portuguese had a re-union in Boulogne, and Sir Arthur Currie was reported to have very considerately proferred our services to Foch, we moved our lines from La Targette to Boyeffles, the guns going to Angres with one section in a forward position near Lievin. There is little of note in our stay there, barring one or two incidents. Boyeffles was rather a home; at first we were all crowded into three Nissen huts, but soon congenial souls began to put up tarpaulins or shacks elsewhere in the orchard. Remember the angry arguments that would arise over the ownership of a battered piece of corrugated iron or a chunk of two by four? There was only one drawback; the lines occupied too little space, the stables and huts forming a hollow square with the wagons in the centre. So that Bert commanded a bird's-eye view of all parts of the Battery at once, and by standing in the lane leading to the street could cut off any trying to slip over to the cookhouse before the "Turn Out !" But, 'twas the Spring of the year, when the flowers smelled sweeter than creoline, the little birds twittered happily from the manure-pile, the pride of every Frenchman's front door, and some young men's fancies "lightly turned to thoughts of love!" Dick Diamond in particular was wont to post away to Fosse No.10 nearly every evening. A regular Lochinvar, but grooms always looked so nice and smooth. Besides, what mademoiselle could resist a soldat who rode a horse while most of them walked?

Major "Reggie" Armitage through his secretary George Edward Cooke sent copies of the daily schedule to be observed at the lines. Harness cleaning was the main item but there was something said about grooming and - oh yes! - dress parades in bandoliers, spurs and gas-respirators. It seems a shame to bore the reader with our frequent allusions to harness-cleaning, but really, one couldn't tell the story of an artillery unit and leave that out. To some this may appear a prosaic and futile pastime, but we know it won the war, glory be! As Hamlet never said, "Harness-cleaning? Ha! there's the rub!"

Not so long ago we heard an eminent chaplain say that "where there was no vision" the men didn't see the necessity of button-polishing and similar rot. Possibly - well, at that rate we were all stone blind, except Bert and some of the officers. Still, we wonder if the reverend divine had ever noted the harness of a French "75" battery, or would he consider the French soldiers less proficient and lacking in "vision"? Gentle reader, should an ex-officer attempt to justify the ridiculous eye-wash and brassoizing that ate into men's hearts more than all the 5.9's Fritz could put over, prithee, poke him - have at him and spare not. For we have seen German prisoners splitting their sides laughing at our harnesscleaning operations and yet we thought ours a democratic army. Should he mumble the old line, namely that men's spirits must be broken by petty tyrannies to ensure good discipline, tell him "Pooh, pooh," and likewise "Bah!" They can get away with these arguments in some places, but there's an old saying "You can't kid the troops." Most of the shining and regimental stuff inflicted on the Canadians emanated from the servile ambition to imitate in all things the Imperial Army. Just as certain of our officers endeavoured to cultivate Oxonian accents and used phrases like these "Oh, I say, Less, old bean!" "Right-o old thing" or "No end tophole!" Rather amusing though now, isn't it?

Well "Reggie" had plenty "vision" and saw that the war would finally be won in the harness-rooms. For this reason some ignorant drivers nicknamed him "Silvo," but Jack Percival called him "Tin." There was another word besides the "Tin" which the reader may supply. Usually after Joe Cox read the longwinded orders of the day, the boys broke into a derisive "Hee-Haw" as they trooped off to stables, but there was no use in kicking against the pricks.

Coming to more serious matters - about this time some red-banded high mucky-muck had to put all the estaminets "out of bounds to Canadian troops!" Those beggars were always trying to knock all the joy out of life. But the British Expeditionary Force canteens had a goodly supply of "Haig and Haig" - for officers.

Good old Bert marches up to the rear position like a hero. A little soft music from the band, please - thanks! The gunners had sweet revenge on him one evening, a merry gibe, as it were. A chain of the fellows were passing ammunition down into a pit and somehow got Bert into the line. By a little manoeuvring they had Bert halfway down the entrance where he couldn't straighten up and he was soon sweating and puffing while his back ached from the continual bending. Everyone worked at top speed to break old Bert's heart. Perhaps if he'd got more of that sort of thing he'd have shown the gunners more consideration when they came to the wagon-lines for a rest.

Upon returning to Boyeffles shortly, Bert swanked around considerable among the bomb-proofers - for had he not seen the guns at last? George Magee, wearied of his vaporizing once quietly interpolated "You were never at the guns, Sergeant-Major." "Like bloody —-, I weren't," roared Bert, his mustachios bristling, "I was at the guns ten bloody well days." "Oh, that wasn't the guns" George came back, "that was only the rear position." Not long afterwards the battery witnessed one of the rawest deals we remember and there were a good many. George Magee, an old original, than whom there was not a gamer or more conscientious worker in the battery was reduced for "inefficiency!" If it had not been such a disgraceful exhibition of either malice or stupidity, it would have been laughable. "Inefficiency" forsooth! A man like Magee reduced, while we were led by virtual children. Little it mattered to George - he was too big a man. But his friends - and they included all the men of the Battery - felt the slight put upon a prince among fellows by some who would never measure up to him. Why at least weren't they honest about their reasons for reducing him - simply because he was above kow-towing and servile fawning and scraping - instead of hiding behind the vague term "inefficiency." But enough, for one gets riled yet in thinking of it.

Suddenly some superintelligent Staff Officer discovered that we were "in the wrong area." So the 8th Brigade was ordered out of Boyeffles and moved into some former Cavalry stables near Carency, known as the Westminster Lines. The Honorable Artillery occupied our quarters in Boyeffles, it is said they were called "Honorable" because they were not paid for soldiering.

Nothing very exciting transpired during the next two or three weeks. "Aeroplane" Flint was hauled away to hospital for the umpteenth time in the mess-cart, also "Duke" Ryan who, in a wild sprint for the cookhouse, sprawled into some barbed wire. That young cherub, Horn, got his hands on Joe Cox's canteen funds, and the Red Hussar's boots. He vanished in the gay metropolis of Mont St. Eloi and ere the hand of the military descended upon him, considerable of the roll had passed out of his pockets to various "Crown & Anchor" boards. For some days Horn had a wonderful time, a comfortable room all to himself, nothing to do but sleep and read, while the guards brought his meals to him. Well, the kid might as well have had his little fling with the canteen funds for all the benefit we ever derived from them. "Reggie" believed the canteen surplus existed solely for the purchasing of Brasso and saddle-soap which was all very nice and thoughtful of him, but - shades of Crosse and Blackwell! - we'd have appreciated a great deal more a few odd vegetables for our skilly, not the "Desecrated" variety either. In due course, Horn appeared before the Colonel, who regretted that he couldn't have the youngster soundly spanked and left him to adorn the feed room of the battery. The punishment meted out in the Army was usually in inverse ratio to the enormity of the offence thus we have seen men tied to a limber-wheel for being a few minutes late on parade or wearing rusty spurs.

There were spirited games of baseball between the various sections or between the "Limers" and Canadian-born. The Red Hussar pitched occasionally, but his Sam Browne didn't prevent the lads from pickling his offerings into the far timbers. "Dutch" Cass banged out a peach of a homer one evening, that landed square on the top of some staff-officer's limousine. If it had only been an open car!

One day the road from Villers-au-Bois was filled with incoming troops - infantry, transport, signallers - an endless procession. We left the stables, grooming kit in hands, to size up the strangers. They were evidently not Colonials and those who could understand English reported that they were part of the Fifth Army who were relieving the Canadian infantry. From long range conversations, we gathered a deal of information about the great German push. Each had a taller story than the one before him, and we got all the sad details, even to the yarn of the "bloke" who swam the Ancre to Albert to rescue a field-kitchen. He must have been awfully hungry. There was much discussion in the harness-room where Jack Percival suggested that a ribbon in running colours should be awarded those who participated in the Marathon from St. Quentin. This, he claimed, would be only following the precedent of the Mons ribbon.

The newcomers appeared later to be very extravagant with their S.O.S. flares and they were always smelling another German offensive. Nearly every day they had reliable information that Jerry was coming over next morning in millions to mop the earth with us. This meant a great flurry at the Wagon Lines, old Bert hunting down the drivers of the gun teams, Joe Cox and the Red Hussar locating their grooms, and the bomb-proofers packing their kits ready for flight. The gun-teams waited up by the guns through the cold night, returning in time for breakfast with mingled feelings of relief and disgust. From posting up the line braced for considerable excitement, its a rude jolt returning with the sad realization that Fritz has put another good one over on you. Not that we were pining for trouble - ye gods, no - but you had a foolish feeling as though "Reggie" Neelands or Hec Cowan had just victimized you with one of their threadbare gags.

Chapter III - 5

Rhubarb And Roses

Towards the middle of May, the guns were shifted from Lievin to Calonne, the horse-lines being back in the little mining village of Fosse 10. While the divisional artillery and infantry were back of the lines in training for open warfare, we occupied a reserve position at almost extreme range - which is unquestionably preferable to "rest" billets when there's a good war on. For in that sector things were reasonably quiet, indeed our guns had to be drawn up to the O.P. to be registered - a unique situation. Beaucoup bombarde to the North of us, encore bombarde to the South - we said "San-ferry-ann" and were quite content to read that the Yanks were winning the war. For Fritz left us more or less alone, beyond letting some imaginative beggars come over and give themselves up in order to kid the Intelligence Department. No wonder Heinie didn't bother us for there were reserve gun positions, trench systems, and barbed wire belts away back beyond Hersin-Coupigny, which accounts also for pictures of French women milking their cows beside "the wire" and staff-officers photographed in heroic poses in a trench.

From a distance Calonne did not appear to have fared very badly in the Great War, the compact vista of red-tilted roofs almost deceiving one into thinking the village was more or less intact. Upon a closer view that impression was soon dispelled, the houses being mere shells with walls blown out and interiors wrecked. More conspicuous buildings, such as the mine-works, were utterly demolished - still, considerable of the village was standing, however war-scarred, and it was not a mere map location as most villages in which our guns had been up to that time. From the slag-heap one looked out over the plain to the German lines and watched our trenches and advanced battery positions being strafed or, more comforting sight, our own heavies throwing up the dirt in the Huns' territory.

The cellars of houses made admirable gun-pits and sleeping quarters and thus the boring work of filling sandbags and dragging of iron rails was more or less eliminated. It was a great change from the musty caves of Thelus and damp dugouts to live in a semi-civilized fashion and the fighting men were

PAY OFFICER
WHO SAYS TH' LUCKY OL' MUD-HOOK?
FRISE

not slow to take advantage of such houses as were inhabitable. Where the ceiling was rainproof, the troops lived on the ground storey, what they sacrificed in bomb-proofness being more than compensated for by the freshness of the atmosphere, and besides, it was like good old pre-war days to open a door into your quarters, rather than crawling into a burrow By this time we had learned that, if a place could not be made 5.9 proof, then the less over your head the better. Others lived under tarpaulins in the lee of an orchard wall- a sufficient proof that the Boches didn't molest us a great deal in Calonne.

It would have been a revelation to any of our friends in Canada could they have visited us there, and they would have gone away feeling a great deal of sympathy had been misspent on the troops. Suppose you were to guide such a visitor through the village during a quiet hour of the day when our heavies were silent and there were no 5.9's landing any handier than Maroc or St. Pierre. True, there were trenches galore running through the village but you could scarcely bluff him into thinking you slept in them with so many inviting airy bungalows still standing. You would lead him through a breach in the wall into a backyard where some of the boys are throwing horseshoes or Ralph Morden trying to pitch sloppy 'outs' to Simpson. Then, entering one of the houses, the tourist would find half-a-dozen khaki heroes playing poker on a salvaged table, others reading shoals of four months old Cosmopolitans or creolining their shirts. Then, you lead him down into the cellar where the old howitzer squats on the cleanly swept floor, every bit of brass agleam, wheels and all dripping oil, the tools nicely tacked to a felt background and the shells neatly piled in shelves. Everything perfect and in good order, as is only possible when you are not firing to any extent.

The same was true of all the quarters there, with slight differences as the inmates' sense of the artistic varied. Every man boasted a bed of either wire-netting or camouflage stretched over scantling, while tables and assorted chairs had been collected from various quarters or rudely constructed. In addition to the orthodox mess-tins, most rooms displayed a miscellaneous collection of chinaware - once the pride of a thrifty housewife but now desecrated with greasy skilly and suspicious bread-pudding. The visitor would likely lose all appetite for supper upon seeing the vessel, in which one of the gunners proposes to draw the crew's ration of tea. The walls of the room are tastefully covered with such intimate illustrations from "La Vie Parisienne" as appealed to the lovers of beauty unadorned among the troops. In the Headquarter's parlour in particular, a ravishing array of stage favorites and movie queens held one's attention. But of course, that fusser Army Howard, had ventured there with his confidential report sheets. So we fear the visitor would depart feeling there was a mistake somewhere, and that the colossal

European conflict wasn't so thrilling after all. And then probably - when well back on the road to Fosse 10 - Fritz would dust him up with long-range stuff to rub it in.

Still we wish some one with a poetic soul could draw a picture for you of those peaceful days in Calonne. Some one to describe the poppies trying to conceal the shell-holes in the fields, the patches of rhubarb that carried on in unsuspected places, the profusion of roses that still marked former flower gardens, and the strawberries which led to the baking of very amateurish but delightful pies. We were but vaguely appreciative of the beauty and fragrance of the flowers but keenly alive to the possibilities of the rhubarb and berries. McAdam, for obscure reasons called by his comrades the Duke of Duck Lake, waged a ruthless war upon the strawberries. When the Duke was through feasting there was nothing to be hoped for from that patch by any one else for weeks to come. He wrought terrible havoc, devouring with equal enjoyment green and ripe, small and large, in the manner of the song, "For they eat 'em tops and all over there!"

There were some heavies in the village and they were too conscientious, breaking in on the beautiful stillness with spasmodic bursts of gunfire. This not only shook down too much of the little plaster left in our boudoirs, but was apt to stir Fritz into a come-back. It seemed asking for trouble. When occasionally Fritz dropped a shell into the choicest rhubarb patch or the basketball court, we were not so much alarmed as indignant. There were acres of open fields to shoot up without mussing our lawns, it wasn't playing the game. Only a Hun would have been so rude as to plunk anything into our luxurious apartments there, but good old Fritz didn't disturb us often.

Orders came through to the Battery Commander to send the two men most in need of a rest to a Rest Camp by the sad, sea waves. Don Ack McArthur, gas bombardier, and Smythe, the battery runner, were elected! The duties of the gas bombardier were arduous, he showed Assistant Wheeler Foster where to tack blankets to the various doorways. Occasionally he took a trip around squirting some solution on the blankets, the formula of which is a secret known only to qualified Gas Bombardiers. This was to annul the poison in the gas, - personally we think creoline would have been more to the point. But aside from the fatigue consequent upon his exertions, we believe the reason Don Ack needed a rest was due to the shake-up his nervous system sustained in a singularly narrow escape. He was sitting one afternoon in the headquarters sleeping apartment, originally destined for a machine-gun post, the walls of which were of reinforced concrete some four feet thick and a roof of the same material, when a shell exploded just outside. If he had been outside the pillbox where the shell landed, he would likely have been injured. Don Ack said the concussion was awful.

This reminds us of a story they tell on Sergeant King - you know, the man Scotty was always asking after. In the middle of the night, back by the plank road in front of Mont St.Eloi, a naval shell ripped out a big hole almost under the sick lines. King nearly had a fit when he saw the fresh crater in the morning, "If it had come twelve hours earlier, I'd have been there and got it."

To create a little interest in Finnerty's cookhouse productions, various forms of athletics were indulged in. A basketball court was fixed up in one of the yards and, when the sun wasn't too hot, the more energetic proceeded to slap each other around. There were a few minor interruptions when the ball went over the wall into a bush of barbed wire, or when the machine-gunner up on the slagheap woke up to blow three blasts on his whistle.

There was very nearly a fatality at a horseshoe tournament one afternoon, the hero being Paddy Ruddy, the wild Irishman who drove the mess-cart mokes. Paddy, who was at the guns for the day as mounted orderly, was a very interested spectator till a horseshoe coming from nowhere carommed off his head. As they bandaged him up before helping him to the Dressing Station, Paddy said mournfully in his Irish brogue "Faith, I always heard there was good luck in horseshoes, but bedad, I'll never belave it again."

After rolling a surprising amount of barbed wire to one side, a baseball diamond had been cleared in a field in the rear of the village and, despite the odd shell-hole, there were good games of an evening. Following a strenuous session of basketball or cribbage, the lads were accustomed to ramble over to the swimming pool in Maroc where two-piece bathing suits were not insisted upon. Major "Shorty" Craig of the 30th Battery chancing to disport himself there one day with the troops, had an historic conversation with a "Jock" who was not aware that he was talking to an officer. For the swimming pool levelled gunner and major and "a mans a man for a' that."

But beyond a doubt the most popular diversion in Calonne, as elsewhere, was draw-poker. Nearly every one became poker fiends for it is the only game in which the greener a player you are, the more heartily you are welcomed to join. If you are a dud - at baseball, you are reduced to the role of the bystander and the same of any other game, but your ignorance of poker makes you all the more acceptable. So the more proficient were enabled to fare sumptuously upon *pommes de terre frites* when they visited the wagon lines, or to purchase *des oeufs* and *beaucoup cognac* in Bully Grenay. The rest waited patiently for the next pay parade and stuck to solitaire.

The study of systematic theology had qualified Andy Lane to get away with numerous bluffs, and, if he can always collect his salary as easily as he collected from the lads, we predict very smooth sailing. But it was annoying to seasoned and veteran gamblers like Charlie Flesch to watch a prospective minister raking in the well-sweetened ace-pots. "Vell, Andy," Charlie

Where Mars Had Passed.

remarked on one occasion when Andy's luck was growing monotonous "You vill soon haf a new orjan for your church, kit!" So Charlie commenced calling Andy "The Poker Pastor" and for some time Andy couldn't gather in the torn bills without being asked "Anoder pipe for dat orjan, kit?"

Rhude and Olds of Don sub were musically inclined and wont to warble in close harmony. They gave a concert occasionally, and probably their best number was the duet which ran "And when I meet Antoni Spagoni, the Torreado-or!" Then Rhude had a very clever impersonation of the illustrated lecturer - "In our next picture, ladies and gentlemen, you see Jo-Jo, the Dog-faced man, commonly called the Anteater, because he lived with his Aunt for three months and never paid her a cent of board. Larry, turn - the crank!" There were a good many other pictures in the course of that instructive lecture, but some of them should not have been passed by the Board of Censors.

During the hot summer weather most of us went around tunicless and very much deshabillé. Riding breeches were discarded for slacks, cut-off about the knee - sometimes rather a bizarre effect being produced by slicing one leg off higher than the other. Puttees were seldom bothered with, unless you were looking for a stripe, in short we dispensed with all the clothing possible. In the Huckleberry Finn costume affected by most of the troops, it was difficult to guess whether a man belonged to the artillery or a kiltie battalion. Ben Case, the Wind-jammer, was up at the O.P. one morning thus ambiguously dressed, and finding time dull on his hands strolled along the trench, field glasses in hand, scanning the front for something of interest. Approaching an English infantryman he innocently asked a number of questions about the lay of the land in those parts. The Englishman became suspicious for the Fifth Army was very apprehensive of German spies and indeed, at this time, there was a reward for the capture of any. So as Ben sauntered off, the Englishman followed him with fixed bayonet and had him brought as a suspected spy before their Company Officer. As Ben was without a tunic there were no badges to show what unit he was in. (probably Ben's tunic had few badges on it anyway!) Naturally with his tunic his paybook was missing also, and most damaging of all, he wore no identification disc. So that while at first, enjoying the joke, he gave confused answers to kid the Imperials along, when losing patience he tried to establish his identity and asked them to take him a few yards away to the O.P., his captors were absolutely unconvinced. So, under a guard of three men with rifles, loaded and bayonets fixed, they marched Ben nearly half a mile back to Battalion H.Q. Here a very peeved Canadian signaller had to wait while the guard ate their dinner, catching fragments of their conversation wherein the astute youth who had spotted the spy, dwelt on the glorious time he would have with £20 and 14 days' leave - the reward offered for capturing a German spy. After a long wait the Imperial Adjutant, with a runner and the aforementioned guard escorted Ben back up the trench to the O.P. as he had suggested in the first place.

By this time, the reader has probably concluded that life at the guns in Calonne was all to the merry and so it was. Let us now wander down to Fosse 10 to inspect the harness and the drivers. It is almost superfluous to say that Fosse 10 was a mining village, for the only name of the place was the number of the pit. Though within range of the German guns, and occasionally strafed, the mine was being worked and most of the miners' families had remained with their homes. The various units were billetted here and there among the civilians, usually a dozen crowded into an attic. The horses were in stables, which ran from one end of a street to the other, so that the French folks passing along had to keep a wary eye upon the mules, who had the habit of lashing out upon no provocation.

The Battery cookhouse was in the rear of one of the houses and when the trumpet blew "Stand to your feed," O.C. Smith and his grimy helpers carried the grub out to the roadside. First they deposited a box full of sliced and buttered bread, on another box lay a pan of warmed maconachie and another of bully hash. You took your choice - either was equally deadly. Next in line stood a kettle of shadow soup, another of bread-and-sandbag pudding and lastly a big kettle of tea. A light breeze blowing up the road wafted dust and even less palatable ingredients into the soup or tea, but we had long since ceased being too fastidious. Soon a crowd of little urchins assemble with mugs or plates, waiting patiently for les anglais to be fed, when they will be permitted to polish off what remains. O.C. - bless his generous heart - let them ruin their tummies with maconachie and bade them "allez toot sweet!" The little queen in the house where our stuff was prepared usually came in for considerable chaffing from the line-up - "Promenade ce soir, mademoiselle?" "Non, non! Vous no bon, jamais promenade!" At which a shout of incredulity would go up and M'selle would retreat followed by parting shots in Andy Brown's Aberdonian French. Sometimes when we lined up hopefully for the same old fare, M'selle would appear in her Sunday-go-to-meeting clothes on her way to Mass. Then the whole battery would shout in chorus - "Ou, la la! Beaucoup swank! Mademoiselle toujours promenade!" But she always took our remarks in good part, probably because she didn't understand them, and we brought her our tunics to sew buttons or patches on and sundry mending. A very neat job she would make of it too, and throw in "the sunshine of her smile" for good measure.

In the estaminet on the corner, A sub lived "like bloody gentlemen." Now we think it was not merely by accident that they elected to spread their blankets out there, for there were several sprightly jeunnes filles whisking about and they could get beer any hour of the day. Though French beer is pretty insipid stuff, it was well worth ordering for the pleasure of seeing "Flatfoot Liz" shuffle across the sawdusted floor with the never-failing enamelware pitcher. Here, almost any evening, you would find half the sub playing "Hearts" and "Tiny" McKenzie shaking the floor with exultant laughter every time he gets rid of the Queen of Spades on some one. Alfie Sanders, whose middle name was "Auction Bridge," would stand a little back of the table, feet slightly apart, knees dipping and ceaselessly tapping the ash from his cigarette in his nervous way. From the attic above come peals of laughter as Bert Alford solemnly announces the Scriptural Lesson for the day from the Second Book of Artemis.

One evening old man Neal entered in a towering rage. He had been away with George Gourley, the canteen proprietor, laying in a supply of brasso and saddle soap for the boys. Now, Neal had a perpetual thirst which had to be quenched at every estaminet along the route, while he handed the reins over to George to watch the mokes. About twenty kilometres from home, Neal dropped into a friendly cafe and must have found agreeable company for George waited in vain for his return. Finally losing patience, George put the whip to the mokes and left Neal to his cups. It was a very wrathful man who emerged from that tavern and found the mess-cart had disappeared. Through the long homeward tramp he nursed his anger and, when he at last reached A sub attic, poured out execrations upon George Gourlay and all his generation. What he would do to that faithless canteen manager when he met him was terrible to contemplate. In the midst of his recital, George clattered up the stairs and looked round in his meek manner. All waited breathlessly for the luckless youth's annihilation. Neal raised himself a little from the floor - "Get out" he roared "get out!" His heart was too full for even his lurid vocabulary to find outlet. George began to stammer something but there was a look in Neal's eyes which forbade argument. He got out.

Neal was quite a character and came to us from the B.A.C. where the bold, bad men were numerous. He had been in the American Navy and travelled widely - you know the synonym for an old soldier! Yet Bert spoke softly to him for he was a man to conciliate rather than oppose. He was not with us long, but occasionally we heard rumors of his stormy career in other quarters. Still, he was an ardent patriot and proud of his American birth for he celebrated the 4th of July by a glorious week-long drunk - a most memorable jag - and no one had the temerity to interfere with his idea of a sane Fourth.

In our poor way we tried to reciprocate the kindness of the people with whom we were billeted. We bought condensed milk, sugar and soap for them in our canteens, pinched hay when they wanted to stuff a mattress and shared the contents of parcels with them. When some madame came to the tap back of the stables for water, there was always a gallant driver to carry her buckets to the house. Often, when we were getting ready to turn in for the night, madame would call us down to the kitchen for some café noir or an excellent salad - this would send some one upstairs on the double for a Canadian cake and so forth till there was quite a spread. Monsieur would tell how he was wounded at Verdun and assure us that the French, Canadians and Scotch were the best scrappers. Often he would come up and look over our equipment and compare it with the French soldiers. It was a treat to see the look of disgust on madame's face when you showed her the bread-pudding you didn't eat at dinner. Then she would give us a plaintive story of how the officers set the drivers to cleaning harness in her garden, concluding with the naive conviction, "Les officiers pas bons, beaucoup swank mais toujours pas compree!" in which we heartily concurred and suggested that she have her kids steal the saddle soap. M'sieu was made a staunch friend by giving him issue cigarettes and you had a real standin with the family by holding the kiddies on some staid old war-horse's back. The youngsters tried to help the fellows around the stables, filling haynets, and trailing feedbags behind them for the picquet - men have been knighted for less.

The army supper very rarely filled that aching void and blessed were those who had the price of eggs and chips in their pockets. We soon learned where the eggs were youngest and the chips done to the most exquisite shade of brown. Usually you had to wait your turn at the table while the grease boiled merrily on the little stove. Remember the old lady across from A sub's estaminet with her unvaried query - "Eggs?-Cheep?-how much?"- all the English she knew, but we had as little French. Somehow eating in their little kitchens seemed different from going into a restaurant now. You felt one of the family, especially when the sticky-fingered children climbed all over you and demanded your cap badge for a souvenir. After all we were only transients in their little village, hundreds of different units had been there before us and, when we left, hundreds more would come among them. Still, for the time they made us welcome and took a real interest in us. Never a driver left the billet to go up to the front at night but Madame gazed after him anxiously and wished him "Bon chance, M'sieu, et bon voyage!"

We remember the day "Sunshine" was carried to his long rest in the little cemetery there. He had been known to many of those kindly people for his cheerful spirit and contagious good humor. There were not only soldiers standing at the salute while A subs' blacks passed down the road with the flag-covered coffin on the limber. In a group of civilians, who watched in reverent silence the little procession, was the girl who waited in the estaminet where he had dined while down from the guns. She was weeping bitterly and we were ashamed of having once called her carelessly "Flatfoot Liz." Yes, they were goodhearted folks. We were a nuisance tramping through their homes, entering and departing at all hours, but they rarely complained. They didn't regard us with suspicion or contempt because we were common, ordinary soldiers, but took us as they found us, and what they could they did for us.

There were as usual frequent inspections of horses and harness in Fosse 10, where the major had the drivers bring their teams one by one to him. It would have been too much trouble for him to go down the line from horse to horse. The luckiest men were the drivers of mules for Reggie did not run his hand under them so freely nor slap them to see if any dust remained on their hides. Before a harness inspection old Bert approached Paddy Ruddy whose team was out every day, the harness consequently being constantly rusty and muddy. Bert knew this, and furthermore that Paddy was not given to hurting himself at cleaning it up, so he inquired "How are you getting along with your harness?" "Foine, sir," Paddy answered, and sure enough he led him within and displayed an irreproachable set, steel glittering and leather well saddlesoaped. Bert, who had been prepared for something entirely different, was forced to bestow grudging praise. Paddy was warmly complimented upon his good work. Later in the afternoon Paddy passed Bert with the mess cart but a most atrociously dirty set of harness on the mokes. Bert stopped thunderstruck - " Driver Ruddy!" Yes, sorr." "Whose bloody harness is that?" "Me own, sorr." "Well, blank bloody blank! I thought you'd your harness cleaned." "Och, sure that was Dixie's Oi showed yez!" And before Bert could find further words, Paddy whipped up the mokes and rattled off. Dixie, it might be explained, was a hardworking G.S. driver, who kept his harness in apple-pie order, and in substituting Dixie's set, Paddy had chosen wisely and well.

As a refuge for the civilian population from shells or bombs, two deep dugouts had been excavated in the village. They looked mighty bomb-proof and one of them was not far from our stables in the road by the school. One night, Fritz was lobbing stuff over at regular intervals, landing pretty adjacent, and Joe Cox, who was in charge of the wagon-lines, left his billet in haste. He stopped long enough by the stables to warn the picquets to remain on their beats and, if the shelling came any closer, to take the horses off the lines. After issuing these heroic orders, Joe hot-footed it to the deep dugout and disappeared into its shell-proof security. Which reminds us of another officer, named Scarth, who was with us for a short time in the Y position at Vimy. While the Battery was firing one afternoon, the odd 4.1's were bursting unpleasantly near and spare parts whining through the air. In the gunpits there was at least cover from flying splinters, but Scarth, from the immunity of the officers' dugout in the bank, ordered the numbers one of the gun crews to stand outside at the back of the pit and acknowledge his orders as it is directed in F.A.T. Needless to say, the fellows had more sense than to expose themselves unnecessarily even to humor him. Rather a contrast from old "Chuck" Lawrence who came down into the pits and swung a shovel the night after A sub was wiped out. He wouldn't ask anyone to do what he was afraid to tackle himself. Unfortunately, Chuck didn't seem to be afraid of anything.

Baseball and football leagues were organized with a team from each battery, the Brigade H.Q. and the B.A.C. "Dode" Wilson captained our team with Jim Rance our sole hope in the box. Our baseball team was like the little girl who, when she was good, was very, very good, but when she was bad... The major is said to have won considerable money the day the lads trimmed the 32nd, at least he treated the team to eggs and chips that evening. Old Bert was a loyal fan and it was quite safe for even the picquets to wander over to the diamond, though after the game, when all trooped back to stables, several horses would be found wandering loose, spilling the feeds or calmly browsing in some Frenchman's garden. Oh, the wild band-waving and parlayvooing when Madame saw the havoc in her lettuce beds! A place on the baseball team seemed to imply a promotion to the rank of bombardier shortly, and the star performers such as Kelly, Fallis and so forth, were retained at the wagon-lines while the old reliables trotted around from O.P. to O.P. We could always bawl out Steve Brodie when he stepped into the box for Brigade Headquarters. That was one team we could beat, but look at the bunch Steve had behind him. Good heads though and it was worth going to the game to watch Tiny Clem's evolutions around first base, or "Baldy" Lewis chasing flies in the outfield and he had plenty to chase. Still Steve grinned and chewed Spearmint. Wonder if he used to pitch for Newmarket? The day of a game was always a sad one for O.C. Smith. After he had carefully counted the slices of bread, some fans from the guns would turn up, looking for a meal, and upset all his calculations.

Our football team was seldom victorious. "Mobile" McGhee was a good fullback, but it was no use his trying to stop the ball with his shins for he couldn't close his knees together. They all tried hard, especially Jack McKen and Saddler Ross, who bumped into everybody. We had a big field day and Sam Murphy, who had got a little inspiration somewhere, was the central attraction in a clown costume. We cannot go into the details of our sporting life in Fosse 10, and possibly some will consider we have devoted too much space to it already, but we would like to say a word at this juncture for the institution which made these healthy diversions possible, the Y.M.C.A. In so many places athletics were out of the question, but where it was possible the "Y" provided the troops with baseball, football and other outfits, besides arranging and supervising field days and tournaments. Nothing did more to take men's minds off the war than engaging in strenuous, clean sports, and we were provided with all the necessary equipment free. Besides fostering athletics, the "Y" was responsible for the little entertainment which we occasionally found in concert parties or cinemas, and there alone we could buy *Canadian* fruit, biscuits and tobacco at a reasonable price. It was a never-failing source of free writing paper and Red Triangle canteens up the line dished out free cocoa or coffee to passing troops. You were glad to hold out an empty condensed milk or even bully-beef tin for the hot liquid. The Y.M.C.A. was no *permanent base* institution - they kept right up with the troops. Not to speak of the "Y's" work in following the last big push, they had a canteen in Vimy village the summer we were there and we could go on citing others. We only mention these things here because we have heard much knocking of the Y.M.C.A's work in France by misinformed or ignorant persons. We had no connection with it and have no axe to grind in defending it, but fellows who were over there know what the "Y" meant to us. The man who disparages the work of the Y.M.C.A. at the front convicts himself of never having been there. There is a kind of chap who always wanted "Jam on it" and the pity is that many people who were not in a position to know the facts have taken their hot air for Gospel truth.

A few more words and we shall have to bid farewell to Fosse 10. We had an innovation there in the location of forward horse-lines in Aix-Noulette. It was a driver's Paradise! They lived in an orchard, free from parades or restraints while the horses had lots of grazing and grew sleek and fat. An ammunition dump in Aix-Noulette went up one night in a tremendous explosion and they say Roberts of A sub was nearly shell-shocked. Unfortunately we had never the pleasure of camping there for a day or two and are unable to write at length of the glorious gypsy life the drivers enjoyed.

But we were not to stay in Calonne or Fosse 10 indefinitely and the time came to move elsewhere. The evening of July 14th, the gun teams drove into Calonne and the guns were hauled out from the cellars, while the gunners tried to find room for all their kit. Bombardier Souster, the O.C. of the machine-gunners, had an anxious time disposing of his weapons and ammunition. His right hand man, "Dope" Richardson, was not to be found. It appeared that he and "Sparks" (the wireless operator) after getting at some of the officers' rum, through being on friendly terms with the Major's batman, had proceeded to Bully Grenay for a farewell blow-out. "Sparks" returned in a dazed condition shortly before we pulled out but Richardson was making himself at home in Bully. After cleaning up on several estaminets, he went out into the street looking for further diversion. A pompous English sentry standing smartly at ease aroused Dope's sympathy. He meandered up to the sentry and tried to take his rifle, telling the Englishman to rest; he, Machine-gunner Richardson, would do his guard for him, but the Imperial, having no sense of humor summoned his comrades and overpowering Dope after an epic struggle they led him away to durance vile. On being delivered to the battery, he was fittingly punished by being made an N.C.O. and told to sin no more.

The following fortnight we shall pass over briefly. After marking time for four days in action near Thelus, the guns went up in front of Arras, the lines being back at Simoncourt. Jimmy Finnerty cooked for us there and you will remember his humorous patter while dishing out the grub. "Will ye hev tea or coffee?" he would enquire as you held out your mess-tin, "all the coffee we've got is tea!" When asked where he was born, Finnerty would reply, "In Buffalo, among the dir-rty Irish!" - but let anyone else take a poke at the Irish and Jimmy was on the warpath. He had the appearance, disposition and spontaneous wit of the son of Erin that he was. He kept an eagle eye upon the "rayshuns" as he called the nightly sandbags of bread, bacon and tinned poison and constantly haunted Lou McMillan with complaints about Allies not sending enough water up. "All the wath-her that came up to-night was two patrol tins full of creoline!"

We were not surprised when word came the afternoon of July 28th, that we were to pull out that evening. The gunpits had just been completed to Reginald's satisfaction and a generous supply of ammunition laid in - always when a position had been made as comfortable and complete as possible, it was time to prepare for a move. The following day we left Simoncourt for parts unknown, quite a number of C sub being beaucoup zig-zag and Charlie Flesch reported missing. We entrained in Aubigny that evening with the usual difficulties in coaxing some of the mokes on board. The bravery of drivers in entering a box-car full of kicking horses has always excited our admiration. After horses and guns were squared away, the troops were free to solve their own transportation problems. Many drivers slept between the horses, their lot being not as hard as it sounds for at least there was hay to lie on. The majority were crowded into box-cars of the "4 chevaux 40 hommes" variety, the officers and more influential N.C.O's travelling in compartment coaches. Charlie Flesch turned up in time to leave with us; he had been to Lillers hunting "greens" for the officers' mess. Some one discovered that the Casualty Clearing Station hospital outside the station yard had some hot cocoa left over, and there was a unanimous rush to fill water-bottles. Most of us were asleep before they stuck an engine in front of the train and in the morning found ourselves at the end of the journey in a strange vicinity, not far from Amiens.

Chapter III - 6

With The Big Push

On commencing the march towards the front, the villages through which we passed were filled with French troops and we were impressed by the obvious absence of the regimental stuff among them that characterized our army. Wagon-loads of unshaven poilus, drawn by one team of undersized horses, careening along the road like madmen, amazed us who had often seen drivers up for office for trotting teams with an empty wagon, why, even the brakeman was obliged to trudge along meekly in the rear!

That night, (July 31st) we stopped in the little hamlet of Cagny and did one hour's grooming. 'Twas ever thus in the good old days. After a light repast we got rid of the dust of the march swimming in the stream where the horses were watered. Some of the fellows decked themselves out in the wardrobes abandoned by the civilians during the German advance and many groups promenaded the village in female finery to the huge enjoyment of the troops. Bert Alford made a very winsome mademoiselle while Sam Hughes escorted her in a frock coat and plug hat. Matthews had affixed a goatee to his face and in carefully selected togs looked the French count.

Before going up the line for what was hoped to be the final and decisive scrap, there was one preliminary detail impossible to omit. Reggie had the troops mustered for an inspection in bandoliers, spurs, etc., and those who were endangering the allied cause by wearing their hair too long, we are glad to say, were suitably reprimanded. Personally, we were grieved that at such a stage in the war on the eve of the last phase of the four year conflict, when shortly the combatants would be locked in a life and death struggle, that at such a time, we repeat, men could be found so blindly oblivious of the issues at stake as to imperil their own and their comrades' lives, - aye, the ultimate safety of the world - by neglecting to rub "Soldiers' Friend" on their buttons or "Nuggets" on their boots. Even the elements frowned upon this muster however, and, as the rain-clouds gathered overhead, Salerne was heard to stammer earnestly, "Send her down, Davie."

Leaving Cagny, the following day, we continued our march and well into the afternoon reached Boves. Evidently the Colonel was suspected to be

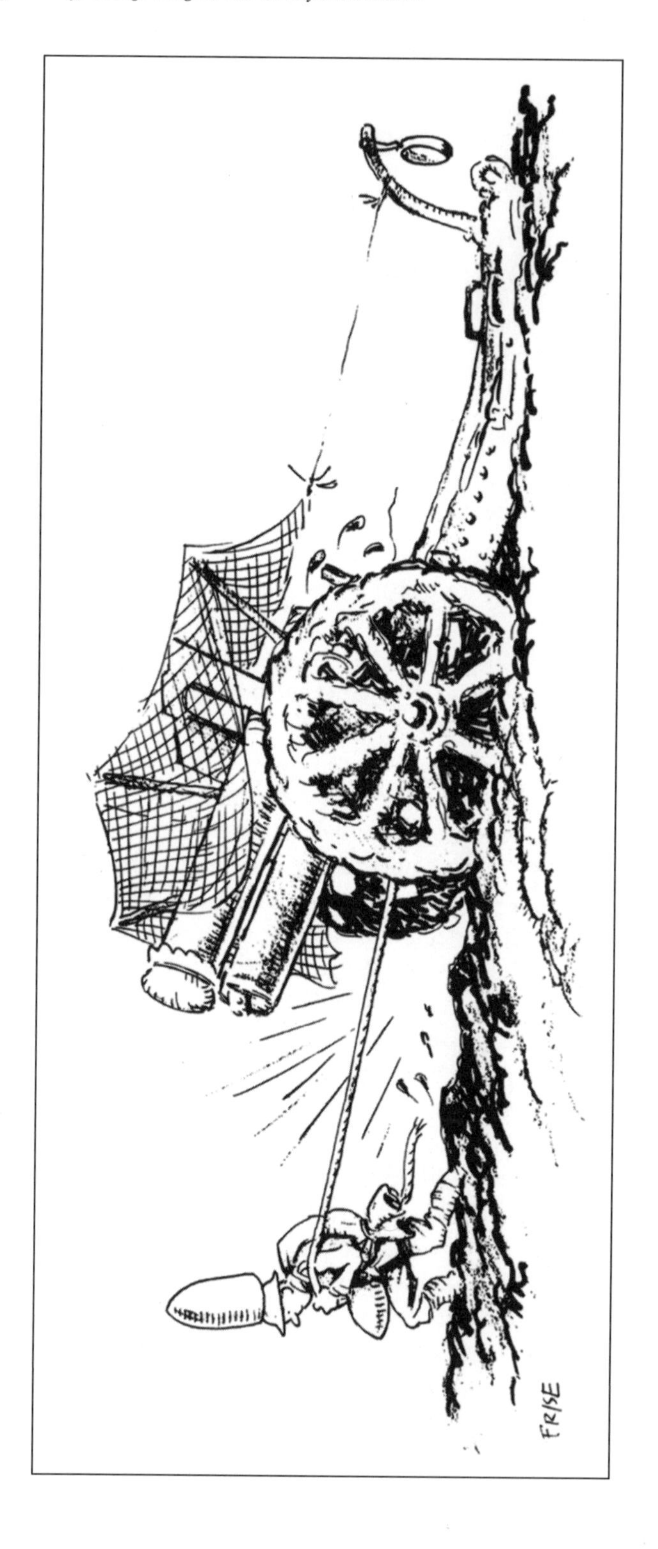
FRISE

lurking here for the order was passed back to ride at attention and "Dismount the gunners!" This order was only enforced by the more ambitious Numbers One but Bert and Leslie did considerable galloping up and down to see that we entered in a regimental manner. "Join the artillery and ride!" - so the recruiting officers once lured men to the Canadian Field Artillery. Mighty little riding we did. You see the procedure on the march was somewhat like this. The battery leaves the gun park with gunners trailing behind the vehicles but, when we hit the road, everyone clambers up on a limber or foot board. Back rides the section commander or Bert - "Only one gunner to ride at a time on each vehicle!" So you jump off. Your next idea is to try to get rid of the heavy haversack and bandolier with fifty rounds ammunition by fastening them somewhere on the wagon or tying them to the gunshield. Soon the eagle eye discerns this unsightly addition to the vehicle and you are reluctantly obliged to put them back over your shoulders. Better that the clumsily swinging equipment should eat into your shoulders than the regulation appearance of the battery be spoiled. So you hike along wondering when the deuce it will occur to those chumps up on the limber to get down and give some one else a chance. If their conscience is not sufficiently tender you suggest that they stretch their legs for a while and leap gladly on top of the piled blankets hanging your feet out over the bale of hay on the footboard.

You are just beginning to feel that is the way to travel when the battery approaches a scarcely discernible rise in ground, a rise of about one foot in a thousand. But the watchful Major sees it - his kind heart considers the poor, fat horses and mules. "Dismount the gunners", - you pretend not to hear but the raucous voice of the sergeant repeats the command with a few added expletives. So you climb down and just as your feet reach the ground you perceive that we are now beginning a downward slope, but 'tis too late! Some one else has blithely copped your seat. So the tramp continues and not unfrequently when they stop - to rest the horses - you are bade get busy harness cleaning and the thoughtful sergeant remembers there are oily rags in the rear limber basket.

It is never worthwhile hopping up on a limber when the battery is nearing a little hamlet. Oh, no, there might be a colonel there or an Assistant Provost Marshal, or goodness only knows what bombproofing majesty. So every one perforce must not only dismount but walk at attention, keeping step forsooth behind the vehicles. Blessed on a trek are the drivers and they receive their reward. There are two occasions on which the buck gunner envies the driver; on a march, or when he wants to ride back to Aubigny for the day. Now, naturally, march discipline is more honoured in the breach than in observance and after a while most of the authorities will get tired of chasing gunners from the wagons but the perpetual pestering made one "fed up" quicker than the mere walking. When you've been hiking along with all your junk on your back and finally squeeze on top of a limber, it's rather irritating to have a spruce officer, who travels on horseback with no weight except his respirator and a water-bottle which does not contain water, gallop up and tell you to get down and foot it. Yet these are the little things one remembers.

Well, we kept on past Boves and up by the left of the woods and on and on. And from the strange route we followed along cow-paths and through sunburnt grain fields we began to wonder if all was well with us. Not that we questioned our leader's judgment - ye gods, no - for the man in the ranks is incapable of thinking, but we'd a hunch possibly the ground didn't coincide with the service map carried by the O.C. Somewhere on the horizon in front, the dirt flew skywards as a 5.9 descended and we were sure it was no place for wagon lines and a sergeant-major. Still we went on in an erratic course until somehow the officer in front discovered we were nearly on top of a French O.Pip. So there was a rapid retreat back to Boves Woods and the battery was drawn up on the edge of the woods which was under German observation. For a while we thought we'd enlisted in a Forestry battalion for they set the gunners to work chopping down young trees with billhooks and army axes in order to clear a space for horselines. But before too many axes were broken and the billhooks had just nicely chipped the bark, the authorities came, as it were, from darkness into a great light and, by its effulgent rays, they calculated that we were in the wrong area - as usual. Sad, sad is the moment when one discovers that the shirt obtained at the baths is crumby, and gloomy are one's thoughts when with two weeks' pay on the "working party" it fails to come up, but darkest, methinks of all, is the realization at the end of a long day's tramp - when all one wants is leave to stretch out somewhere and sleep for centuries - that the O.C. has lost the battery again.

At such a time we doubt if even Rolph Morden's philosophy would stand the strain though we remember his stoic acceptance of the unkind Fates on a former occasion. 'Twas back on Mont Noir, where we lived in a very unsubstantial bivvie, consisting of two rubber sheets and a blanket. We returned one night from braking an ammunition wagon in a pouring rain that came down in buckets, and found our home absolutely flooded by the deluge. The bivvie looked very dejected and on the verge of collapse but from underneath protruded Rolph's legs under the soggen blankets. We thought he must surely be half-drowned and tried to recall the First Aid appropriate in such a case, but, on peering in, his cheerful face greeted us. As we stooped in the entrance we bulged the rubber sheet. A cascade of water rippled down the back of our neck and we cussed with honeysweet words. But Rudolf raised a deprecatory finger and a wan smile flitted across his water-logged features as he quoted "Sweet are the uses of adversity, which like-" but that was as far as he got!

So we restored the billhooks to the limbers and hied us to another quarter of the woods and, after the evening devotions of grooming, we put up tarps or heaved our kits into the remains of former French shelters. Next morning, in an incessant downpour, Bert had everyone out building harness-rooms but about dinner time, when the work was more or less finished, we were again found to be "in the wrong area" and new lines were selected a couple of hundred yards away. The guns went up the line that night.

The following days were busy for everyone and we need not remind you of the night-long sessions packing or slugging ammunition. The night of the attack the battery lay outside Hangard and those who prowled around in morbid curiosity will have stories to tell. It was an evil-smelling locality. Shortly after stretching out to sleep under the guns and wagons, orders came to prepare to move forward, for we were then considerably in rear of the advance. The teams were hooked in and the fellows waited with their few belongings stowed away or on their backs. The minutes passed into hours. Still no orders to move came and the tired troops lay down alongside the vehicles. While thus sweetly reposing Sergeant Barnett's horse evened up old scores by stepping lightly on the Black Prince's face, thereby considerably softening his rugged features. He was in a very chastened mood most of the following day.

Now far be it from us to attempt to trace the footprints on the sands of time that this here 43rd Battery left between Hangard and Warvillers or Parvillers or Vrely or Caix and other burgs. For just as our evolutions and revolutions, advances and sidesteppings were a continual mystery to us then, so they remain a sealed book now. But we solemnly assert and hereby reiterate that our wanderings were considerable and frequent and it will save us a great deal of trouble if the reader, when explaining the battery's share in the Amiens drive, will take a good-sized war map of that sector (one can be had from any demobilized lieutenant, for they treasure their maps as rubies) and let his young hopefuls gaze thereon and when the oldest, John Neuville St.Vaast Smith, picking a place at random, enquires "Was you there, papa?" say "Yes, my son!" - for the chances are you were.

To us, military tactics and strategy - praise be - were as "Million Dollar Mysteries," the why and wherefore of our comings and goings were cloaked in impenetrable darkness, for who can fathom the workings of the master-minds that say to a battery commander - "Run your guns up into the support trenches tonight," or "Stall around Vrely for a week or two." We knew only

what was going on in our immediate neighborhood and often very inaccurately of that, and the arrival of mail or a cigarette issue were more vital matters for contemplation. The second day of the advance, we heard that the Canadian cavalry were through Peronne and First Division H.Q. in Roye. Another day brought the rumor that the British had captured Ostend from the sea. Then when all these wild rumors were punctured, came the inevitable disillusionment and so we took small stock in the progress of events. For is it not written, "Hope deferred giveth a pain in the neck and a dirty mess-tin impareth an odor of Maconachie to the tea." So you will see that we are not qualified to give the military details of these operations and it remains only to discourse a little concerning the way in which the new style of fighting affected us, "who never could know and could never understand."

Honestly, it was a most perplexing war down there, sometimes you wondered if you were at the front or manoeuvring around Hankley Common. Other times you were absolutely certain you weren't at Witley! We scarcely know how to describe it to you but they called it "open action" and, if you look up the chapters in F.A.T. dealing with artillery procedure in the open, you will get some idea of what it is not like. F.A.T. is a great book to feed officers but rarely put into practice, unless the chapters on grooming. You see, we didn't advance with or without dragropes, No. 2 doubling to the head of the pole, a couple to each whipple-tree and the rest assisting on the wheels. No, we'd a few horses and mokes kicking around and preferred to let them do the advancing. Nor did we kneel while working the gun or preparing ammunition - oh, no - if there were any causes for kneeling we'd be flatter than pancakes or streaking for the better 'ole. There are other minor discrepancies in F.A.T. which we need not dwell upon but the worst of this galloping into action in the open business was the difficulty in keeping track of your kit.

It's all very well to laugh about it now but there was a time when that sloppy roll of blankets and dirty sox wrapped in a rubber sheet was mighty precious in your sight. Well, look at the way this open action business balled things up. Suppose your kit was strapped to the first line wagon limber. After the gun-teams have gone back you wait anxiously for the arrival of the first line wagon. Anon appear the ammunition limbers pilotted by some corporal. Are they the first line? No such luck, they're firing battery. Will the first line wagons be up tonight? No, the first line wagons will not be up to-night. Will they be up in the morning? No, Bert will send up the firing battery again, so that the first line wagon teams' harness will not get dirty.

To this day our heart is wroth over the sad fate of our kit, for it was dear in our sight and contained three Canadian issue blankets, - you know - the grey kind with the nice broad red stripe pattern. It was in those novel days when occasionally the wagon lines were only a few hundred yards from the guns and, after one of those dashes forward of the battery ensemble, when we looked for our blankets - they were not. Some gunner had chucked them off to be on the safe side. We decided to go in quest of them. A short walk across the field brings us to the guns where they have everything packed ready to move. We enquire for our blankets. "Well, there were some buckshee ones but we were ordered to reduce our kits and threw a lot into that hole over there." There are blankets in the hole but not ours. Torn, sawed-off wrecks, that a moke would resent beneath his saddle, but we must take a couple. 'Twas a cruel war! Ancient were our blankets and possibly in need of creoline but they and all within them had been ours, - a part of our personality as it were.

But what we objected to most in this open stuff (speaking for ourselves only) was the absence as a rule of deep dugouts and the sad necessity every night of digging a little trench to sleep in. For we were seldom long in the same place while the push lasted and this nightly business of digging a funk-hole became a bore. Remember how about sunset every fellow grabbed a shovel and got busy digging down or widening a trench if any happened to be around? Ah, them was the days! Fritz had little come-back during the day at first but he was hostile at night and mighty careless where or how often he dropped his tail-board. Like Johnny Porteous when he shoved his "smoke-wagon" into an Imperial's ribs-"Say, guy, Ah'm plumb keerless with this thing an' when she starts Ah cayn't stop it."

However, to get on with the war, when things simmered down we loitered around Vrely for a time. Occasionally Fritz speeded us up but that's another story." Here Nemesis overtook Perkins, the heartless trumpeter who had so often evoked our maledictions, for one afternoon, ere he expanded his chest to blow "Come to the stable all ye who are able," something hit him in the arm and he left for "blighty." Now with all due respect to Perkie, a willing gunner and skilful warbler on the trumpet, we are ashamed to confess a sneaking feeling that the only good trumpeter is the one in hospital (provided he got a cushy one). Did his passing do away with reveille? Alas, no, for Bert unearthed some other musical prodigy. The study of that form of music should have been suppressed ages ago. It's a barbaric noise - especially early in the morning when the dew is on the rose.

We had another casualty down there; he didn't make "blighty" but remained to make an efficient battery of us. If the war had lasted longer perhaps he might have. "Major R.S. Armitage - wounded -remaining on duty." The cuticle of one finger was pierced by a shell fragment, but, though he could have gone down the line and possibly reached one of those palatial private estates consecrated to wounded officers, he chose rather to follow the stern path of duty and lead us on to victory. For this he did not receive the Distinguished Service Order.

The sunny August days went by and now we must be on our way for George needs us elsewhere. Nothing in our sojourn in that sector became us like the leaving of it. Through the moonlit night we retraced our steps over the rewon territory, finally halting back in Hangard on the slope of the hill where the German line had run. "The time?" - about 3 ack emma. A bright moon shines through a heavy ground mist that blurrs figures even at a short distance. It is very still for we are out of the beaten track of traffic and in the damp atmosphere the orders of N.C.O.'s to get the horses off the lines to water sound unusually clear. Bert calls, "Gunners take some bloody buckets and help the drivers." Meanwhile some are stretching the good old tarps over the guns and wagons and turning in to snatch some sleep before morning. The horses are watered and fed, surely all is over now to woo Morpheus "What's that? An hour's grooming? You're crazy, man, the horses are wet with perspiration and dew, and yon luminous orb proclaims 'tis still night." "Come on, out of it, out of it! Everybody to stables and carry on with the grooming." "By whose orders?" an incredulous sergeant asks. "The major's orders," is Bert's only comment, as he goes to the next tarpaulin.

A few short days back that hillside had been ploughed with shells, and bullets sang over men pressing forward to root out the curse of militarism and its attendant evils. In those shallow trenches others had perished in the defence, as they thought, of their Fatherland. By that scooped out hole yonder, where empty cartridges still strew the ground, a husky German machine gunner had lain beside his gun, repeatedly bayonetted and his head crushed in. At the bottom of those dugouts by the sunken road lie what had been men before Mill's bombs bounced down the steps. Over in the field to the left of the wood were the ghastly remains of Frenchmen mowed down in rows in earlier fighting for Hangard, but why dwell on the scene? In and around that demolished village the dead of three nations rest. There is something eerie still in the air, even the hardened soldier feels it. It is a cemetery.

Once more that battle-scarred slope is alive with soldiers. Oh, battered church of Hangard, from whose tower machine-guns swept the Canadian Mounted Rifles, saw ye ought more pitiful that other August morning, when men had died like soldiers, than these who, coming through one mill and on their way to another, pat at wet horses' flanks with curry-combs! See the horses shaking their feeds impatiently on the picquet ropes stretched from limber to limber, and men, impotently cursing, making a pretence at grooming them when grooming is impossible. Only one man in two has a brush or comb, does that make any difference? No, the rest are slapping the astonished brutes with their hands. Behind the lines walk section-commanders to see that the major's order is carried out. They cannot express their opinion as that angry driver who mutters "And they say we're winning!" What could have inspired so asinine an idea? Search us, we can only say with Polonius "Oh, this is the very ecstacy of madness!" There is much that fortunately we have almost forgotten, much we would fain forget but, wherever two 43rd men come together, this will be recalled - the night we groomed by moonlight in Hangard-en-Santerre. We venture to append the following with profound and most abject apologies.

"And the pale moon rose up slowly and sadly she looked down
Upon that awful battlefield with grooming brushes strewn.
Yea, calmly on that dreadful sight her bright beams seemed to shine -
How they'd have laughed at Bingen, dear Bingen on the Rhine!"

Everyone is familiar with the story of the Canadians' share in the closing months of the war, only leaving one quarter to strike in another. In all we freely take off our hats to the infantry who did the dirty work, but the artillery contributed to some extent and the 43rd was kicking up a racquet somewhere during the various engagements. Here our story will appear very meagre but it must needs be so, for we were moving so often and generally busy that we have only a confused remembrance of those days. To some it may appear exceedingly incongruous to slide over the Amiens drive, the fighting before the Drocourt-Queant switch, the fall of Bourlon Wood and Cambrai in a few paragraphs while we write pages about a little spell out on rest. But when we cannot remember anything out of the humdrum everyday strafing or being strafed, we prefer to pass on - knowing that a summary of the various positions occupied and that sort of thing would be most wearisome and unacceptable to the fellows of the battery. Possibly the very few incidents which we shall mention may recall the surroundings to the reader.

You remember the position we were in for a time after leaving Monchy - up near Boiry, wasn't it? - where the guns were down in the field near the stream and we all slept in a trench further back, where "Red" Ashton had an awful time trying to cook for us. You will remember also the two deep dugouts at the head of the trench, occupied of course, by some Brigade Headquarters and occasionally by us as well, when Fritz got too familiar. One night the aforesaid Fritz was acting a little gay and throwing them over far too adjacent for comfort, so the majority of the troops made for the dugout. Down there was peace and security while thirty feet overhead there seemed to be a war on. Just as the fellows had found a place to squat and were groping for cigarettes, came sounds of a strange commotion in the shaft leading down. Jim Rance burst into view, breathless and eyes popping out of his head, while behind him rose a slithering, scraping noise as though a piano were sliding down on its ear. "It's a horse!" Jim gasped, "It's a horse!" There was no doubt about it at all for the next instant the mounted orderly's fiery steed skidded across the floor and anchored up against one of the bunks. It was customary there to keep the horse out of sight in the trench as much for our safety as its own, and the poor brute, frightened by the exploding shells and doubtless hearing the voices down in the dugout, had instinctively sought his natural protector, man. Jim had decided to go below at the same time, but barely made the bottom first, and from the horror-struck look on his countenance and the rumpus behind him, one would have concluded the whole German army was at his heels.

We left there suddenly one night and pulled in off the Arras-Cambrai road some distance in front of Vis-en-Artois. There was all-night work getting ready to contribute to the morning barrage but at zero-hour the battery was found to be out of range. We were not there long and all we remember is the old German tunnel we occupied under the road and the novel spectacle, the morning the Canadians entered Dury, of old Frenchmen and women riding back from the front on artillery limbers or in ambulances. Liberated after four years under the heel of the Boches, who can imagine their feelings as they were taken back through the Army to Arras? Through the disappearance of "Slim" Cottle, the officers were minus a chef and dependent on the tender mercies of the gunners who were cooking, as our hash-slinger, "Red" Ashton, had also vanished. It was noticed that they suddenly became very interested in the troops' rations - Leslie Wright being particularly solicitous and enquiring as he angled for a hand-out, "What have you got for dinner, boys?"

Eventually we were relieved by the 36th Battery and went behind the lines for a rest. A rude surprise awaited us in Arras on our way out for, though the Germans had been pushed away back from Arras towards Cambrai, they could still reach the city from Mericourt way. We had forgotten that however, and were rumbling along quite at ease, feeling absolutely removed from the war and anticipating a spell of utter relaxation from the necessity of keeping an ear open for "tout-suiters." But, as we neared the Gare du Nord, suddenly without any warning a rubber-heeled naval shell whistled overhead and exploded in the street below. We could scarcely credit our ears but there's no mistaking the rush of a shell and, to make assurance doubly sure, another hissed over a little closer and, as the drivers whipped up the horses, that old familiar, pungent smell of arsenic fumes met our nostrils. From peacefully sauntering along we were now burning up the road in good style and the major didn't seem to be worrying about the appalling bad form of a battery trotting through a town. He set a ripping good pace, in fact. Now Bert had a good steed, well groomed and tended and capable of a pretty good burst of speed, but it couldn't fly fast enough to suit Bert's palpitating heart or else he felt too exposed in the saddle. At all events, he abandoned his horse for a limber and made himself small on the footboard. The dauntless Harry Chace bravely rounded up the deserted quadruped - Bert says it ran away from him and possibly this feat paved the way for that glossy enamel-ware thing Harry wore later on his tunic.

We were not long back in Simoncourt but the battery barbers were kept busy cutting our hair and thereby hangs a tale. Dick Wright had the honour of trimming Leslie Wright's locks and, as he clipped and snipped, Leslie enquired "How is it you gunners always seem to have lots of money, I always see you coming out of estaminets or eating eggs and chips?" "Well," answered Dick, as he violently shoved the right section commander's bean 44°30' more left, "it's like this, most of us gunners - excuse me (as he misses Leslie's ear by two hairs breadth) - have means of our own. We're not dependant on the army for a living like you lieutenants!" Leslie was too busy spitting out a mouthful of hair to reply so we don't know whether he swallowed this (we mean Dick's explanation) or not. But Leslie's surprise, upon finding that some of the "other ranks" had a few francs to spend, reminds us of a little story concerning Samuel Price, the hair-restorer analyst.

Now, back in the wild and woolly west, Sam was some pumpkins, almost a potentate one might say. Long miles of golden grain submitted to his binders, the cattle on a thousand hills were his; when he put a few paltry thousands into Victory Bonds the DeLisle Squeak blazoned the news to an admiring world, yea, and among the Grain Growers' Association the name of Samuel Price was spoken with bated breath. But hearkening to the call of his King and Country, Sam left his fertile acres and learned to groom horses in the Canadian Field Artillery where his bank account excused him from no more fatigues than the most impecunious among us. So it came to pass one summer day, while the battery was in action by the Double Culvert, Vimy, that two Young lieutenants fell upon us from a clear sky. Peculiarly significant were their names - Green and Pilgrim - for truly pilgrims they were and green. Now, an officer never travels light, for he doesn't have to tote his junk himself, and the nocturnal ration-wagon groaned beneath their accumulated kits while behind it stalked Gunner S. Price in the role of brakeman. On arriving at the battery, the two subalterns emerged from the shelter of the officers' mess, heroically flashing their electric torches in search for their collapsible canvas wash-stands, etc., before such trivial things as rations could be thrown off. To the huge delight of the drivers, one of the youths, after Sam had rolled off their kits, said grandly "Here, my man!" and tendered the opulent Sam, the wheat king of DeLisle - half a franc! The humor of it struck Sam as he climbed up on the seat later and held up the coin between his fingers and remarked whimsically, "By the great horned toad! To think I could buy them and their fathers out six times over and never feel it."

Soon the battery went up the line again but we shall pass over that Canal du Nord business, our pilgrimage around Bourlon, Raillencourt and St. Olle, as being purely war staff and very dry reading. If you crossed the Canal astride the gun-barrel or clinging to the camouflage on the trail, we don't need to jog your memory; as for Bourlon its only redeeming feature was those piles of shavings that made the ground softer to sleep on and the less said of St. Olle the better. As the French say, we were "a little there." Somewhere in the shuffle we lost "Red" Ashton. They say he went away shell-shocked, asserting that he was shy two perfectly good legs. But we shouldn't be surprised if he merely put one over the Medical Officer as he did on Joe Cox once at La Targette. "Red" was in the officers' mess then - in a culinary capacity. This enabled him occasionally to sip sparingly of that fountainhead of courage, "Haig and Haig," until Joe, noting with alarm the frequency with which the mess cart had to be sent to Hersin-Coupigny, sought to keep tab on the consumption by marking with a lead pencil on the label the point at which he had left off. But "Red" was not to be denied by so simple an expedient and the next cold morning, when upon replacing the cork he saw the tell-tale pencil line high and dry, he rubbed out Joe's cargo-line and some inches lower recorded his own objective. When Joe went to refresh himself after superintending the mornings grooming, the bottle looked to be at low tide but the pencil mark could not lie, so, though there seemed to him to be "something rotten in the state of Denmark," he asked no questions of "Red," who was raising an extraordinary amount of smoke from the fire.

Well, Fritz pulled out of Cambrai and he says it was "according to plan" and others claim the Canadians chucked him out, but we believe he evacuated the bally place because he couldn't stick the wailing of bag pipes that filled the long suffering air when the 51st Highland Division drew nigh. So we moved over to the left and while the guns went up to Epinoy, Joe Cox lost the battery trying to find the contemplated horselines. Dark was the night and chill - still they rumbled on and after some hours aimless wandering Joe decided to consult Leslie Wright. What hope! The column came to a halt and waited impatiently, knowing that some one had blundered yet again. "Have you got a map, Les?" "Yes-er-have you got a light, Joe?" And somewhere in the darkness a "fed-up" voice groaned, "Oh H—l! If they use the map we're out of luck for sure!"

One night when "Lulu" Walsh went up with the ration-wagon to Epinoy, the cook was not on hand to unload it. Lou McMillan was raving and tearing around and finally got the rations hauled into the cookhouse, a little haste being imperative owing to the odd shell. A very blasphemous Lou McMillan there found our old friend Jimmy Finnerty calmly and methodically shaving! Lou bawled him out hotly; why hadn't he been around to attend to the rations? Didn't he know there was a war on; what the deuce did he mean dolling up while drivers and horses waited around for blighties? Jimmy shoved his tin mirror back into his haversack, then he looked up - "And how could I come out wid me face all of a lather?"

It was getting on towards the end of the war though we didn't know it, for by that time it was hard to imagine it ever quitting. Still there were evidently grounds for suspecting that Fritz would retire any night from the Sensee River and all units were kept on the qui vive for a German withdrawal. On one occasion, when everything had been packed up preparatory to a pursuit of the supposedly fleeing Huns and the teams were hooked in to the limbers, it was discovered that Fritz was after all still doing business at the old stand. Whereupon "Baldy" Lewis, the Brigade adjutant, telephoned the various battery commanders in this vein. "You can put your little old Ford back in the barn. There'll be no joy-ride to-day!"

However Fritz did slip back and it was like the miserable beggar to do it at night so that we had to get up around two o'clock or some unearthly hour. One seemed to have just gone asleep when somewhere - "Tah-dah-de-dah! Tadadedadeda-ah!" There's the 24th trumpet - and the 30th! Now what the Sam Hill are they celebrating? Hope to goodness our trumpeter has more sense! Oh, that queered it - and our own cherub, after several preliminary toots, joins the glad refrain. So we arose and walked. Ah, distinctly we remember, it was the day after payday for as we stopped on the road, awaiting further orders, someone started a little game and, when we moved on, we

remember wishing they had postponed that joyful event. Thank goodness the Sensee was neither wide nor deep for the mokes didn't have much confidence in the pontoon bridge thrown across by the Engineers.

We were only a day in front of Aubigny-au-Bac, when we were ordered to relieve a Fourth Division battery somewhere to the left. We were on the road most of the day but at nightfall there was still no sign of any artillery in front of us. We kept hiking on. It was a very strange night, very still and quiet and no one seemed to know where either the Germans or our own people were. The villages through which we passed, though deserted, kept looking less and less battered and bore little trace of the war. To our surprise, as we entered one town, lights were to be seen here and there and we heard scattered cheers and women's voices. It was probably the greatest moment of the war as we passed down the street, the women, old men, and children yelling themselves hoarse and waving long-hidden flags. The gunners tramping along came in for considerable kissing but, better still, many of the people ran out with some sort of scones, rather tough to bite through but very welcome at the time. It was a never-to-beforgotten night. For the first time the end seemed in sight and all were infected with the pent-up joy of the civilians who had seen the last of the Huns retire that morning. We cannot give any idea of the general excitement, the excited French folk yelling "Vive les Canadiens" and the fellows calling to each other "Old Fritz is —- now!" There was the same enthusiasm in each succeeding hamlet and we finally stopped for the night in Somain. The people acted as though they couldn't do enough for us, and crowded around, often staring at us as though we were from another world.

We pushed on the next morning and got within reach of the 5.9's again. As the battery went through a village usually the road was found to have been mined and detours rendered necessary. When the column was halted by a huge crater, the old men and children could be seen working like mad throwing in stones and debris, trying to expedite the passage of the guns. Immediately after the last German outposts had withdrawn the civilians had got busy filling in these holes and we heard of one case, where an old man, who had started to work with a shovel just after the mine had been exploded, was shot by a Uhlan. As the guns bumped across, the excited people waved us on with very expressive pantomine of what they would have done to the Boches. At one point an old Frenchman, probably a veteran of 1870, who had been busy with the others repairing the road, stood stiffly at attention, with bowed head and hat in hand as the battery passed.

Our cookhouse wagon frequently got into difficulties and considerable chaffing was directed at the drivers - Paddy Ruddy being on the lead team, Tony Perkinchilli, a passenger on the centre and Isaac Cooke wrestling with the wheelers. When they were stalled for the umpteenth time that day, Bert implored them, "Pull together there! J.B.C., pull together!" Quoth Paddy, "Faith did yez ever see an Irishman, a Dago and a Jew pulling togeth-her yeff!"

Eventually the brigade was relieved and we rested a while in Wallers from which place our right section and the 30th Battery left for Habarcq where an Artillery training school was being opened. After the souvenir section had left for "college" the fighting portion of the battery started on the last big march which most of us consider the best part of the war. It was not long before we came upon the civilians again and you will remember how, as soon as you entered a house or what was left of one, madame would fill up the never-failing coffee-pot and set it on the stove to boil. The "café" may not have been up to much, being mostly a mixture of burnt barley and chicory, with sometimes a lump of sugar thrown in if they had any left. However it was the best they had and the sharing of it made us feel "right at home" with the family.

Just after crossing the Belgian frontier we came to the "House of Mystery," where we were not met with the same enthusiasm as back in France and we fancied we could detect at once the difference between the two races. We were not left long in doubt as to the reason. At the moment of our arrival, sober-faced civilians were just removing the last murdered victim from the house and there were plenty of signs within to indicate that Fritz had held high carnival. Naturally the Belgians were not inclined to speak about what had happened in those blood-stained rooms, and we never learned the real story of the tragedy. Nevertheless, when the beer was mopped from the floor and things squared away, it began to look like a home and the last word in comfort was spelled when someone discovered potatoes and flour upstairs. Fortunately there were several stoves in the house and, after the regular army supper, the job of preparing a real feed began. According to taste or expediency potatoes were fried, boiled or roasted while Jim Rance and Deruchie made flapjacks all night the way they used to up in the bush.

After all had eaten to their heart's content and pipes or issue cigarettes were going strong around the kitchen stove, Skeen, the battery canary, treated us to such old favorites as "An Old Fashioned House" and "Sweet Adair." He had just returned to us after the Goddess of Fortune - or was it the sergeant-major? - had ceased to smile upon him back with the Concert Party. Then "Limer Jim" Davidson told how "Snuffy" Gordon and Joe Cox had hunted all over the country for some outfit which they couldn't locate. In his own peculiar style "Snuffy" cursed the war, the map, the lost battery and finally Billy his horse, who had a habit of rearing just when "Snuffy" had his finger on the exact spot - on the map. In the end, he decided he didn't want to find the battery anyway and brought his party in.

We had just got nicely settled down to sleep when orders came in for us to take the road again. At such a time the Sergeant-Major's lot was not a happy one. The drivers were scattered all over the town and for a long time not even a copious and steadily maintained stream, of profanity, directed up and down the street, was sufficient to root out all the drivers of the gun-teams. Eddie Madden drew down the curse on himself and all his generation when he innocently enquired, on his way to the lines, "How's she going, Sergeant-Major?" The only explanation of such a Faux Pas on Eddie's part was that at such an unholy hour it was a question as to whether it was still "the night before" or "the morning after."

While all this was going on, the gunners were packing up the guns and E sub delegated Mark Everitt, who was temporarily attached to them for discipline and rations, to stay in and cook the potatoes that they had peeled for breakfast. Now above all things, a fitter is supposed to be a practical man and in leaving Mark behind they felt assured that everything would pass off according to plan.

All went well until he was leaning out the window to drain the spuds when Mark "pulled a bone" and let the whole works go. When the hungry gunners came in, all they found was an empty kettle and a very sheepish-looking fitter. Pandemonium broke loose but above the racket you could hear the famous Pee Wee Island slogan from Bob Laird, "Go way! Go way! for Heaven's sake, you old dope, you old dope." It was not till Armistice Day that Mark was allowed to forget it, at which time he retrieved himself as we shall find out later.

In due course, the last subsection was turned out and we were on our way. As we sat half asleep on top of a jolting ammunition wagon or slugged it along behind, we regretfully turned our thoughts back to the smooth bed we had just left behind on the stone floor of the House of Mystery. Or perhaps, we wondered how long it would be before we could turn in between the white sheets in that little old bed back home.

From now on the war had hardly touched the towns and with us it was merely a question of who got the best billet, i.e., the house where the prettiest girl lived. We all spoke our best French and in some marvellous manner were understood. "The Ox," who by some means or other had got next to the rum-jar, came wild-eyed into a house early one morning after an all night march. "Bon joor, madam, compree cushay?" "Mais oui, m'sieu!" "Then would it be alright to sleep here to-night - comme ça?" he added with a dramatic wave of his hand towards the floor. Madame compreed and "the Ox" had a billet.

Up towards Jemappes our advance became a regular triumphal procession known as "Shorty Craig's Circus." Belgian and French tricolors appeared as if by magic from their hiding-places alongside fairly good imitations of the Union Jack made from odd bits of cloth. The entire population lined the streets singing "La Brabanconne," "La Marsellaise" and even "Eets a long way to Teeperaree." One old lady, some distance off the road, finding she couldn't run fast enough in her wooden clogs, took them off and came running across the field, brandishing her sabots in the air and cheering with the best of them. The fellows marched along arm-in-arm with the girls and it is said that even such hardened old campaigners as Dunc Irvine and "Weary" Beattie submitted to being kissed right on the public street, too! We met a constant stream of refugees, old men, women and children, some carrying all their worldly possessions on their backs, others wheeling barrows or hauling carts plied high with mattresses, bedding, kettles and often an odd chicken coop. They couldn't tell what might have befallen their homes but they were going back and that was good enough for them. Those were indeed great days to live in, and the hardships of the last three or four years seemed to us to have been well worth while.

When the news of the Armistice came through to us on the morning of the 11th, it seemed hard to realize it was all over. The guns were lined up ready for action in a little field and to all intents and purposes it just seemed an ordinary day. There was a cheer or so from a few scattered groups of soldiers and civilians but, some way or other, we didn't seem to be able to workup much enthusiasm.

It was soon doped out that the last shot from the battery had been fired by Tom McCarthy who had just "enlisted" again after his usual summer in blighty, where he was reported to have swanked around *with a wire in his cap*! Like this man Caesar who divided all Gaul into three parts, Tom campaigned in Britain during the summer, returning each year to Gaul to hibernate. He had some difficulty in locating the cartridge case which had been salvaged by a civvy with ideas of his own about souvenirs and it required all Tom's Irish eloquence to induce him to part with it.

A few of the boys who still had the odd franc left, were lucky enough to get hold of some bottles of wine which had been hidden for over four years for just such an occasion but most of us through force of circumstances were even denied that luxury. A party was being organized to represent the battery in the triumphal entry that "The Staff" were staging for themselves in Mons - but we couldn't see it that way. Mark Everitt, who was one of the aforesaid lucky ones, figured he wouldn't mind walking the other way but going to Mons would be taking him two miles further away from home. When told that Mr. Cox's orders were that he should go, he expressed our sentiments by telling the Acting S.M. what Mr. Cox might do, adding "And tell him that Fitter Everett said so!"

Tales reached us later of hilarious doings on Armistice Day in Paris and London - how "Nonnie" Brackett auctioned off cabbages on the Strand; how Murray Munn balled things up trying to direct traffic on the Boulevard des Italiens and how Hairbreadth Harry, according to his own modest story, cleaned out, single-handed, a whole barroom - full of Yanks who admitted they had won the war. But such glorious deeds were not for us - at least not on that day. After dark that night, we moved up through Mons in a drizzling rain and came to the village of Nimy on the northern edge of the City.

Chapter III - 7

Apres La Guerre!

The preceding chapters have dealt with the epic achievements of the 43rd Battery on many a shell-ploughed field - and whale-oil fragrant harness room. But now with the aid of the Portuguese Navy and the American Expeditionary Force, the war is over and won so that we would gladly refrain from inflicting further particulars upon the reader, leaving the troops to wander around Belgium feeling "all dressed up and no place to go" - as indeed they did at the time. However, there still remain a few bloodless battles to record for the glory of Vimy and Passchendaele was enhanced, nay, even eclipsed by conquests in Nimy and Grez-Doiceau. "Peace hath her victories no less renowned than War" and the hobnailed boots of the 43rd shall yet re-echo o'er many an estaminet floor or clatter in unison with *sabots Belges* in moonlight promenades ere we get the blighters demobilized. So at the risk of tediously prolonging what we fear has already been unconscionably lengthy, we shall devote a final chapter to the battery's adventures "Apres la guerre."

For the benefit of those who do not speak French as fluently as ourselves, we venture to explain that "Apres la guerre" being interpreted is "after the war" - although the words had acquired a deeper significance than that during the years between. That is, since it was generally accepted by soldiers and civilians near the front that the blooming war was going to last indefinitely, "Apres la guerre" came to mean a time that would always be in the future, in short "never"! Let us illustrate. When the quarter-master indented for your new tunic, you could expect it "Apres la guerre"; when you requested a bottle of vin blanc on a credit basis, Madame would assent cheerfully, "Oui, apres la guerre!" or if you asked the belle of Gouy-Servins, "Promenade ce soir, M'selle?" she would make you happy with the same vague promise "Apres la guerre." Trusting this is a lucid explanation we'll get on with the war - or rather the peace.

Now that the war was *fini,* our numbers began to be greatly increased by "old soldiers" wandering back from hospital, leave or school. As each returning prodigal was gathered to the fold, Weary Beattie, now known to

BULLY BEEF
FRISE

the natives as "Monsieur le Fatigué" took upon himself the task of jumping on these slackers for absenting themselves during the last great push. Weary went on leave from here himself with full regimental equipment as usual (including a cartridge-filled bandolier, spurs, water bottle and mess-tin). Unlike Steve Brodie, Weary never believed in taking a chance but then Steve got hit and - what is more - took it sitting down, but that's another story. We are told that Weary spread such a great line about the "advance to Mons" to our budding officers in the Beaver Hut that they regretted ever leaving the battery. His leave was up on Xmas day but again rather than take a chance on staying over, he left the Big Smoke the day before and ate his Xmas dinner travelling "deluxe" in a box-car in France when he might just as well have enjoyed it in the Regent Palace.

From this place short leaves to Brussels were granted and all enjoyed themselves according to their individual tastes and inclinations. Old Bert announced that a fine quality of beer was available there at a moderate price and hence, as cities went, Brussels ranked second only to London in order of merit. Some took in the cabaret life and turned night into day with wine, women and song; others again visited the churches, museums, horticultural gardens or art galleries and reported the time of their young lives. "Scotty" MacLean sighted a "gr-reat" team of white oxen the moment he stepped off the train. "Och," he exclaimed reminiscently in describing his trip later, "they would go 1,700 apiece sur-re" - and while he was counting the number of barrels of beer they were walking away with, he lost track of the other fellows! Consequently he had to spend most of his time alone, wandering into many strange and diverse places but, canny Scot that he was, he reached home with money in his pockets which was more than anyone else could say. Sammy Murphy even had to pawn his "British Warm" to stay the full time!

Well, we shall always retain pleasant memories of the month spent at Nimy. The morning was usually whiled away in brisk exercise - rides along the tow-path of the canal, while the rest of the day (except for stables) might be passed sociably in the houses and estaminets or on a trip down to Mons. We soon learned to revise our estimate of the Belgian people, formed in earlier days around Ypres where we had been consistently "done" by Flemish profiteers. The people here more closely resembled the French in speech, manners and temperament, and soon we were "bons camarades" with all. When finally we had to pack up for the trip towards Brussels there was mutual regret and they told us they would "jamais oublier les Canadiens!"

This journey was in the main uneventful, save that Sammy Gordon, who went ahead to select our billets, didn't always give satisfaction. Indeed, on our arrival in Grez-Doiceau, where we were to spend most of the winter, things didn't look very promising and 'Shorty' Craig told Sammy that he could at least say one thing for him and that was, he couldn't have done much worse! However, when we got squared away almost everyone, even the employed men, were satisfied with the prospect.

Those funny marks above are to indicate a break in the story but, had we inserted them at every point in this history where we'd "made a break," the printers would still be scouring Toronto for asterisks. We are merely giving warning to those unfortunate warriors who were not in the Right Section that the following pages concern that "fine body of men" alone and they may skip over the story of our college days in Habarcq. Old Ben Case has questioned the advisability of recording in a battery history the doings of one section apart from the, as it were, harmonious whole. He submits that the work of the Right Section in hastening the end of the war at Habarcq is not one of sufficiently general interest to warrant its inclusion here. Had it been the left or centre section which had gone to school, we would admit the justice of Ben's contention but we insist that where the Right Section, the pride of Leslie Wright and the victor in a hundred harness-cleaning competitions, went - there was the 43rd Battery! In this connection we are reminded of a story of one of our ancestors, a certain MacLeod.

Now, MacLeod was a doughty chieftain of some barren isle of the Hebrides and it came to pass that he was storm swept upon another island where he fell among his clan's enemies, the barbarous MacLeans. But MacLean, strange to relate, didn't chop off MacLeod's head to decorate his castle gate, but gave him dry kilts and set a sumptuous meal of salt herring and porridge before him. And when MacLeod seated himself at the lower end of the festal board apart from his foes, MacLean called magnanimously, "MacLeod, mon, come awa tae the head o'the table!" But MacLeod rose to his full height and said with Highland pride, "Whaur MacLeod seets, there iss the head o` the table!" So we assert that it was the 43rd Battery that followed Leslie to Habarcq - the remnant trailed "Shorty" Craig to Mons!

Our old friend Dugout Dick, now a Colonel or something like that, was principal or dean of this college and we heard that he had a very remunerative position for George Edward Cooke as Q.M.S. George wasn't so stuck on his job in a few days - it consisted merely in keeping tab of the bottles of spirituous liquors imbibed in the officer's mess. This proved a task beyond even Isaac's powers of calculation, but we are running ahead too fast.

There was very little work and that was still further reduced when we were given working parties of German prisoners. What a glorious sergeant-majory feeling it gave you showing the beggars where to start sweeping - just like an unconfirmed bombardier! They did everything for us from sweeping out the billet to grooming muddy mokes - but you should have seen them laughing among themselves when the drivers set them to cleaning harness! And how they could eat! If there were any with more voracious appetites than the German prisoners they were the 43rd under-graduates who lived over in one of the huts by the Chateau and contrived to visit us at meal-time to get a real hand-out.

Our mail was long delayed in reaching us there which occasioned much discontent, still there was little to complain of and indeed most of the lads seemed in good humour - at night anyway. We were glad that "Tiny" Mackenzie's jovial spirits didn't bubble over too often, for one night, when he felt the world was particularly fair and bright, he entered with one "Whoop" and leaping roofwards brought down about thirty feet of scantling. Insisting that the fire required kindling, he was endeavoring to shove this little stick through the stove and up the pipe, when half the hut grappled with him and assured him the home fires were still burning.

Our hut soon boasted all the comforts of home. Under the supervision of Bill Leslie, of trench mortar fame, electric lights were installed by German electricians. The bunks which had a habit of letting certain portions of your anatomy sag through them, were repaired with burlap. Numerous benches and tables were constructed. The latter were originally intended for eating upon but a loftier use was found for them. Carefully covered with saddle-blankets, they were utilized by devottes of the national pastime long into the night and the cheerful voice of Wilfred Kimber might be heard saying resignedly, "I'll call you on principle," as he looked at "pat" hand with two pair in his own. Always an optimist, our Wilfred. Early in his career as a poker-player he had caught some one bluffing and he has been calling 'em ever since. After a run of hard luck Lou MacMillan spent long hours fashioning and polishing souvenirs from old cartridge cases, the sale of which to the opulent Leslie Wright enabled him to again resume the more serious occupation of drawpoker.

All was hushed in the hut one dismal rainy night, even the most inveterate gamblers had long since played the final hand of show-down and were wrapt in slumber. Now and again the stable-picquet entered noiselessly to shove another stick in the stove and to doze drowsily till the tattoo of hooves upon corrugated iron summoned him to separate fractious mokes. Suddenly the door banged open. One or two sleepers stirred fitfully. In the next moment things began to happen to the carefully piled firewood near the door. First isolated sticks clattered down, terminating in a grand finale as the whole structure collapsed in a magnificent avalanche. A few more sleepers sat up and rubbed their eyes. From the centre of the hut, numerous mess-tins left by their owners ready for breakfast, rattled in protest as something swayed against the table ere table and all went down. "What the - came the

Familiar Scenes in Grez-Doiceau.

unanimous roar from the double-tiered bunks. "Who the - is that?"— and fifty hands reached for the good old army boots at the foot of their blankets.

A figure stood framed in the flickering light that emanated from perforations in the stove, a bandolier-encircled figure that balanced itself with a rifle and clutched at the swinging stovepipe for further support. "Fearnot,"spoke the intruder in reassuring, if somewhat thick, tones, "fear not, I am the sentry." A chorus of hostile remarks and pointed hints to take his sentinel activities to another realm were serenely ignored by Gunner Prendergast of the 30th whom the fortune of war had delegated that night of all nights to guard against any civilians running away with the gun-park. He had been lonesome out there, and, though he had blundered into the wrong hut, he was not for voyaging further in search of company. Every Spud Island entreaty to "Go way for — sake!" was to him as a "Welcome" door-mat. He tarried with us and his come-backs soon had everyone turned from wrath to laughter. He confided to us how he had "tossed" the sergeant and the other luckless guards for the combined rum issue. It was superfluous to tell us he had won.

"But do you know," he said, "I'm the unluckiest guy in this gallant army. Three years out here and I never got to hospital, never got a blighty. If it was raining soup, I'd be there with a fork. Say, if I had the luck to get 'napooed' and was on my way to heaven, I'd get brought down by an 'archie!' Here I am, doing guard over a lot of vehicles out in the rain," he concluded as he subsided comfortably upon a bench. "Why in blazes aren't you out in the gun-park then?" came a sarcastic query. "You're a — fine sentry, you are! You should be marching around the vehicles." Prendergast laughed pityingly. "I didn't march around 'em. I stood in the centre and watched them go around me."

Some thirsty revellers leaving an estaminet one night paused with one consent and gazed upon the numerous kegs of bière or vin blanc which lay in the yard. It was so simple! Here lay the solution of those dry nights, immediately preceding pay-day. Carefully selecting the largest and most promising looking barrel, they rolled it up the muddy ascent to the hut. In the process, their clothes were hopelessly plastered, some had sprawled into the "goo" in futile clutches at the rolling barrel, others had got under its path. But all were happy in the consciousness of a task well done. Soon petrol tins, dixies and even canvas buckets were produced and held "at the alert position" to carry off the precious fluid. The bung was finally knocked out by the steadiest hand in the party and a rich, leisurely flowing liquid was disclosed - tar! Among so many barrels more richly laden they had picked out a "dud." So there it remained - abandoned in the mud outside the hut - a monument to blasted hopes and well-laid schemes that went a-gley.

Shortly after the New Year the Souvenir Section was ordered to rejoin the brigade up in Grez-Doiceau. Leslie Wright and Tom O'Neil, who had been up there trying to trace our Xmas mail, returned with glowing reports of the wonderful time the troops were having there and the weekly passes to Brussels. Immediately the majority were anxious to be back with the rest of the 43rd, though some of us were quite satisfied to stay in Habarcq. We couldn't see how there could be any joy in life where Bert was.

So we left Habarcq one afternoon, much to the sorrow of "Blondie" and other profiteers, and after entraining at Duisans were soon jolting along towards Belgium at nearly a five miles per hour clip in the inevitable box cars. Alighting sleepily in Wavres the second morning of the journey, we proceeded to Grez, where "the old, familiar faces" greeted us with caustic comments on our slacking in Habarcq while they were ending the war. It was great though to be with the old gang again and we looked forward to serenely happy days in Grez-Doiceau. As we saw drivers and gunners in the doorways of their billets, leaning familiarly upon buxom Belgian damsels, "Ah," we thought, "here is life at last! After our privations during the great war and in Habarcq, we shall here sit us down to sip pea-soup and watch the village belles trip lightly o'er the cobbles in their dainty sabots till George sends us home." In the midst of this reverie we heard a voice - strangely familiar "Blank Bloody Blank! Dismount those bloody gunners!" - and we knew it was not so to be. Bert was with us again. That queered it - absolutely!

Twisting cobbled streets running from nowhere in particular into the Square or marketplace, a few unpretentious, meagrely stocked shops, numerous cafés, a church and the Hotel de Ville - there was nothing about Grez-Doiceau to distinguish it from countless other sleepy villages in that part of Belgium. On the edge of the village was an imposing Chateau, with beautiful grounds surrounded by a moat, the property of some Count likely and occupied by the Brigade Headquarters. Something of the quiet, sequestered life of the inhabitants was reflected even in the appearance of the place, for there were no mine-shafts, factory chimnies or other signs of industry in jarring contrast with the countryside's quaint, old world simplicity.

We cannot say too much of the hospitality of the friendly folk among whom we were billetted during that winter in Grez; nor shall we soon forget the good-humored madame who, in spite of her own numerous household duties, found time to darn and wash our clothes. One morning after bringing madame sundry sox, she completely mystified us by inquiring, "Chemise, M'sieu?" and then it dawned on us that the good lady meant our penitential army shirt. But it had never occurred to us before to think of it as a chemise. To us the word "chemise" had always called up visions of filmy trifles light as air but our old army-issue shirt - no, our imagination couldn't go that far!

It was enough of an evening to sit around the kitchen stove while madame prepared wonderful salads or fried potatoes, and how those good dames could disguise bully beef or even O.C's mysterious preparations! One could not enter the house without madame pressing a cup of black coffee upon you and the boys all bragged about the quality of soup the old lady at their place could put up. Do you remember Madame's consternation when, while she was stirring the seething potage, you dropped in a few Oxo cubes and assorted "Gong Soups" for luck? The problem of the winter's food supply didn't seem to have the least effect upon these folk's generosity.

In a certain kind old body's house, Rolph Morden resided after returning from an hilarious leave in southern France and they say he came back raving about a "dream girl" in Cannes, the very memory of whom moved him to flights of poetry. Although Rolph was wont to sit dreamily perusing Oliver Lodge's "Reason and Belief " with his free hand absent-mindedly dropping every two minutes to a fast-disappearing box of chocolates, still, at the table he was a gallant Trencherman and kept madame busy replenishing his plate with vegetable soup. When urged to a third or fourth helping, Rolph would airily wave his bands and exclaim rhetorically, "je ne refuse jamais, madame, je ne refuse jamais!" So that once when madame's keen eyes noticed that Rolph was making short work of 'Weary' Beatty's chocolates, not understanding that parcels were common property in the army, she thoughtfully took the box out of reach and apologized to Weary later for his depleted stock. "Pauvre Rudolph!" she said, shaking her head knowingly, "je ne refuse jamais!" Not long afterwards when Rolph, who, had meanwhile come to suspect that his "je ne refuse jamais" was becoming proverbial, was proffered the soup-dish for a second issue, he refused with great dignity. "Oh, Rudolph," exclaimed madame in mock surprise, wagging a playful finger at him, "pour la première fois!"

Everyday G.S. Wagons set out for Hamil, ostensibly to bring fuel for their billets but many loads were sold on the side to ready buyers between Hamil and Grez. At a very early period in our sojourn there, blankets and spare kits began to disappear and gradually everybody woke up to the fact that almost everything we (or the other fellow) had, possessed a fair market value. It was no uncommon sight of an evening to see chaps slipping out laden with surplus belongings and peddling their wares among the farm houses and while the cooks undoubtedly had the best graft of all, still very few were long broke in Grez while they'd an odd pair of sox left. The guns and wagons were stripped of everything that was saleable and leather trappings, saddles, oats, shirts, jerkins, sox, blankets, even horses and mules - all went for the one purpose - to provide the wherewithal for a few days' fun in

Brussels.

Because of this and also because nothing better could be found for us to do, we began to have a real regimental guard. Every night at six o'clock we fell in down by the cookhouse in charge of a confirmed or an unpaid bombardier with our buttons and boots shined, rifles cleaned, and we submitted ourselves to be put through our paces by the S.M. and the orderly officer. In this respect Sid Williams seemed to us to be a little too conscientious and paid more attention to details than we thought necessary. But then he had only been married on his last leave and no one could tell how long we might be in that neck of the woods, so we couldn't blame him much. It depended largely on the bombardier what sort of a guard was kept. Some were newly appointed and anxious to please, others had already been balled out for losing a horse or a bag of oats and these held strictly to the letter of the law. But, for the most part, we were fedup and the night was spent by all concerned in uninterrupted slumber until we were awakened by the picquet just before reveille parade.

Xmas day was the occasion of the biggest and best feed we had demolished yet, not excepting the banquets at Aubigny and Ohlain. The expenses were met by some of the profits of the Canteen fund, the raw materials having been brought all the way from Paris and cooked to perfection in the village bakery by one Hill. Sad to relate, old Bert was not among those present. He took the count early in the day and was found before dinner lying *hors de combat* upon the orderly room floor. Tender hands lifted the unconscious form into a wheelbarrow and the little procession struck out across the village square and up the rocky road to his billet. What a fall was there, my countrymen! Those fiery eyes, before whose baleful glare the stoutest hearts had quailed, were closed to the beauties of that sunny day; that puissant hand, which raised aloft had checked the course of a battery thundering onwards, trailed helplessly on the cobbles; cap awry, with dishevelled tunic unbuttoned, the man who "had a rank" was trundled to his quarters by rear-rank gunners as unceremoniously as the line orderly shoots his barrow up and down the stables. Only the fierce, waxed mustachios had escaped the cataclysm to mark "the glory that was Bert!"

The dinner itself was a signal success. The menu comprised everything from soup to nuts, including roast turkey and goose with dressing, plum duff, oranges, and finally rum punch! As the day wore on, our spirits soared higher and higher and Major Craig became visibly affected so that words failed him. The Colonel rose to the occasion and, standing upon a table, supported on one side by Tony and on the other by Hairbreadth Harry, came across with the speech of the day. He referred to the time when we would soon be "tous

la même chose" and told the boys if ever they needed help not to hesitate to look him up - "although," he added in parentheses, "I don't know how the —- I will ever be able to do it!" The festivities were closed with a Grand Ball in the Hotel de Ville attended by all the girls of the village and "there was a sound of revelry by night!"

There were a few parades even in this Paradise though the Right Section evaded most of them through living in the far end of the village and reveille was simply a matter of slipping down to the stable and feeding the chevaux in time to reach the cookhouse before O.C. had dumped the tea-kettle into the drain. After a dress review in bandoliers et cetera at 9. a.m., we sallied forth on wild exercise rides up hill and down or, if the roads were too slippery, in some poor villager's field. While madly charging around the field with truant mokes hee-hawing by their lonesome, the incensed farmer occasionally appeared to remonstrate but his selfish whims were usually treated with the contempt which they deserved. Did he expect that our steeds should be allowed to pine away through lack of exercise, merely because he wanted to raise a crop on that field the following Spring? The odd muster parade was held for the reading of orders, when Bert was in the seventh heaven making the flanks of fours prove. Quarter-Master Sergeant C.W.P. Curzon stepped proudly out upon parade one day with rather a self-conscious air, wearing one of those underslung belts affected by Red Caps and other non-combatants. This was too much for Simpson, who called out in real concern, "Hey, Percy, your braces have slipped down!" In the laugh that followed this shaft, Percy's cheeks blushed to an even deeper peony red. There was a day when the lads called C.W.P.C. "Rosie" - before his control of the rations gave him the bulge on them!

When troops are billetted in private houses it is difficult to keep them earning their $1.10 a day - there is too much cover. What is the use of the fuming sergeant rushing into one house to pry rebellious gunners away from the stove if the operation has to be repeated in umpteen other billets? The futility of this was apparent even to Bert and the afternoons were graciously ordained half-holidays. We have referred above to the gun guard each night and in addition there was a picquet and at intervals a brigade guard. Picquet was rather a joke in Grez. The chap on before you stood out in the street and threw rocks at your window till you reluctantly stuck your head out into the cold night. "You're on, he'd yell and disappear to his feather bed. If you were conscientious you arose; if you didn't care a hoot about the liberty of the small nations, you stayed where you were till your shift was up and then woke some other chap and, incidentally, all in his billet. Some neglected even this formality. Less fortunate were those who kept watch and ward over the "criminals" down in the Brigade clink. It appeared as easy to escape from there as Toronto jail, the fugitives usually being recaptured later in Brussels. Most of the fellows though were in for trivial offences and we have our own opinion of the officer who ran for office old original "307s," without a mark against them during three years service, because they returned a day or two beyond their leave.

One night while bravely tramping back and forth with loaded rifle in front of the little outbuilding that first served as a jail, we assisted in a little romance. It was about the witching hour when the orderly officer might be expected and we were walking our beat "in a brisk and soldier-like manner" when two demoiselles timidly approached. We ordered arms smartly and the bolder informed us that she would fain see one "Beellie." We tried to steel our heart to her entreaties but this touching devotion made us relent and suppressing our stern sense of duty we opened the sinister prison door. "Any of you chaps answer to the name of Billy? There's a Jane out here with a bottle of beer and basket of eats under her shawl." The prisoners unanimously sprang to attention but the lawful claimant was sorted out, his pal insisting upon parleying with the other girl. Telling them not to make it a lifetime, we considerately turned our back upon the stolen interview. From unmistakable sounds behind us, we surmised that "Beellie" et al. were making good use of their time. At last, however, we felt called upon to end this affecting scene and with the glad news that "Beellie"' was to be free the following night, the girls reluctantly withdrew with black glances at the unfeeling guard. Bill was equally ungrateful but we admired the loyalty of the girls who had not forgotten their friends in durance vile and reflected there was something in that waltz song "Love will find a way!"

The fussers among the troops were given to beaucoup promenading and it cast a pang into your lonely heart, as you stood on the bridge at midnight after a night's dissipation at crokinole in the Y.M.C.A., to hear the girlish giggles and squeals in the wake of some gallant. Many were the balls, official and otherwise, wherein the village belles were initiated into the fox-trot and one-step and there was not enough floor space for all. "Watty" Walker and some others pirouetted around with more vigour than grace but the girls didn't object to their ankles being walked over. The officers gave a select ball and report hath it that the lads intimidated the jeunnes filles from attending by threatening to cut off their supply of chocolate bars so that the officers waltzed with the maidens' mothers. The accepted custom appeared to be for the youth who had taken a girl to a dance to monopolize her all evening - but who are we to comment upon the way of a man with a maid? However, there was not nearly enough material in Grez to go around and many were forced to ride far afield to Hamil or Wavres or Gastouche to find their affinities. The N.C.O.'s had a big advantage here for they could take a horse at will but even then the path of true love was not always smooth. Jim Rance went around for days swathed in bandages after a fall from "Ribbon" to the cobble-stones.

The hero of all the harness inspections was "old soldier" Knox. Though John was a confirmed grouser, as his red chevron entitled him to be, still his harness was always in apple-pie order on the fateful day. He lived with an old couple and madame was certainly far from comely to look upon but she enjoyed exchanging pleasantries with Jack, who would make very disparaging comments with the air of one bestowing compliments. As the old lady understood no English this was quite harmless; but a visitor felt rather embarrassed. "Gosh," he would remark with a courtly bow to madame, "look at the fine set of teeth she has - both of them!", while madame beamed in absolute ignorance of what he was saying. Once John very debonairly led two old maids, who lived up the street, to a ball in the Hotel de Ville but basely deserted them for the liquid refreshments thoughtfully provided for the perspiring dancers.

The Brigade Concert Party, who were excused from all military duties, in order to, devote full time to the study of the dramatic arts, graciously consented to appear before the public - the nominal sum of one franc being charged for admission. It was considered a mark of distinction to be able to boast a female companion and, not to be outdone by Army Howard, we rashly bought tickets for madame and her two white-haired boys. The good lady was as excited as a debutante and, after scouring the youngsters from head to foot by the simple process of standing the little cupids on a chair and distributing several pails of water over them amid much yowling, she arrayed them in their Sunday-go-to-meeting best. She herself was becomingly dressed for the occasion with a white shawl over her ample shoulders. Madame leaning tenderly upon our arm, the young hopefuls skipping in front we set out for the theatre sincerely hoping we wouldn't run into too many of the lads on the way.

Once within the hall, the kids broke away but later madame descried the rascals perched precariously on the edge of the balcony, and from time to time during lulls in the music waved a menacing fist towards them. Our three piece orchestra kept the house whistling till the curtain rose on the performance and the shining bald head of Fallis was seen bobbing spasmodically to the rythm of "When the Sun goes down in Dixie." Lieutenant (acting Adjutant) Donnelly gave a masterly interpretation of a negro comedian - he acted so naturally - and Bill Fletcher surprised those who had heard that he once enlisted in the Salvation Army, by the alluring way he sidestepped and palpitated round the stage. Enough for the concert - we laughed from start to finish and that's what a concert party is for. After the close, Kelly, and the other home-destroyers with their blushing consorts, proceeded to clear the floor for a dance. We took the family home.

Thus the winter wore on and the fellows by making their own fun amused themselves more or less but all were impatient to see the last of foreign parts and get back to Canada as soon as possible. So it was a red-letter day in the history of the battery, when, after the guns and vehicles had been turned in at Wavres, we presented our horses and mokes to a Fourth Division unit. We wished them joy of the blighters and if any felt a parting pang their grief was well concealed. A driver would pay a more fitting tribute to the horses, for, as Bert will testify, we had no yearnings to minister unto them, but more than once we have regretted since that we were not more patient in our dealings with them. A horse had not even the privilege of grousing, the safety-valve of a soldier's discontent, but perforce had to endure all in silence. They were not to blame for the tedious hours we spent with curry-combs upon them - candidly we believe they were as fed up with being pestered during stables as we were. So here's to, you - Coon-Eye, Funny Face, Windy or Nuts - and you too, our long-eared friends, Dago Queenie and Babe! We've forgotten the times you stepped on our toes or broke the picquet ropes at 2 a.m. - do you forgive our endearing words and lustily

Last Days - See'Em Smiling.

applied stable broom on such occasions!

After the mokes were torn from us, it was only a matter of a few days till we left Grez-Doiceau. During the interval the lads were busy filling out numerous forms which comprised all their personal history, such as-previous occupation? Number of wives and children? Great-grandparent's nationality? Religion, if any? - and other essential data. Then we all filed applications for a two hundred acre farm in Ontario in the hope of qualifying for the Provincial Legislature. There were vehement debates as to which class would be demobilized first, the married men and farmers expecting the preference and those of us who had no status whatever sadly looked forward to clearing barbed-wire and emptying sand-bags for a few more sunny years. Then, after a final kit inspection when all were issued the things they had sold to the civvies, we were drawn up in the square early one morning in full marching order. Our good friends of Grez-Doiceau were out in force to bid us "Bon Voyage" and now and then a fair mademoiselle darted through the ranks to kiss some warrior adieu. In this ordeal, we wish to record as our opinion, that despite the handicapping panoply of haversacks, bandolier, waterbottle, etc., etc., the favored ones bore up most nobly. Then the brigade swung out into the road for Wavres, whistling "Quand Madelon" and stepping out jauntily for at last we were headed in the right direction.

One last, long jaunt in the box-cars, sitting with feet hanging out the doorway or on some one else's kit, jumping out when the train stopped to fill water bottles, trying to locate the cookhouse car, the confusion at night when thirty fellows tried to find floor space for blankets, the protests of the chap whose face you filled with your feet when you tried to stretch out - these and other features of travelling in France you will remember. The second day the train passed through the devastated belt of the old war zone and already it was difficult to realize that amid such surroundings we had formerly considered ourselves fairly well off. The post-armistice recruits collected souvenirs. In due course we reached Le Havre and after the usual route march found the Embarkation Camp where we were to remain longer than we had expected, but, if we had not been chafing with impatience to get on that liner, the time would not have been too tedious.

In that luxurious moment in the morning when, from the cosy warmth of your blankets, you looked out sleepily upon a cold, bleak world and wondered who would have the pep to start a fire in the stove, the door of the hut swung open and an icy blast swept up the floor. A form stood in the doorway. 'Twas Bert with the day's meal tickets. "Out of it, out of it, or you'll get no —- meals to-day!" Profane appeals to close the door and put his tickets to another use failed to move Bert, for he had discovered it didn't pay to go in and distribute the tickets to the chaps as they lay in their warm blankets. If he did no one would show a leg till breakfast was nearly over, so, he made everyone come to him. There was nothing for it but tumble out into the cold and dash for the door in your — well, after that it was just as well to stay up and dress!

Fatigues were almost unknown and, at that, those who helped the W.A.A.C's peel spuds over in the officers' quarters expressed a willingness to volunteer for duty daily. You might, however, be called upon for picquet duty at night to show returning stragglers from Le Havre the way home. Andy Lane forgot to turn up for the "Fall In" the night he was detailed for picquet and found himself up for office in the morning. This after three years without a mark - so you may infer that Reggie was still with us!

After spending two weeks in Le Havre we filed on board the boat one evening and crowded to the rail for our last grimpse of France. Landing in Weymouth the following morning, we entrained for Witley and alighted that night at Milford in a drizzling rain. There was the usual delay in getting started, much lining up, advancing a little and then irritating halts in the darkness when you pitched into your neighbour in front and the fellow alongside lowered his kitbag on your toes. At such a time, when men are anxious to get somewhere and discard their equipment, these dilatory tactics evoke caustic sallies - "How about hit?" "Get the map!" "And they say we won the war!" "Let's go!" "A little life for pity's sake!" "Section commanders to the front! Report when the rear is fed-up!" "We know the way if you don't! But eventually we reached the camp and having drawn numerous blankets were soon snoring peacefully.

After a few more papers had been duly filled and various inspections, we were sent away for seven days leave, most of us having a very slim balance to our credit. That morning, as Bert fell us in for the last time, he didn't seem to care much whether we were dressed properly or not and indeed acted so good-humoredly that we were inclined to think we never properly understood him. Possibly in this story we've not shown Bert in a very favorable light and we sometimes may have been a little hard on the old boy. We haven't forgotten how regularly he turned down our applications for a pass nor his disapproval of our grooming tactics and this may have biased our opinion of him a little for we've a vindictive nature anyway. A sergeant-major can't be popular - to keep in right with the officers he's got to be in wrong with the men and if he were in right with the men he'd lose his job - so we should have let Bert down a little easier. After all, as a rule, his bark was considerably worse than his bite - but he did have an awful bark! By the time we've as little hair on our head as Sam Price, we may have forgotten his withering glare and sleep-disturbing "Out of it!" Who knows but we may

Home Again!

yet learn to revere his memory? Meanwhile we have too painful recollections to indulge in any fulsome flattery - so Adieu, Bert, we bid thee "a soldier's farewell!"

After our return from leave, we lingered a few days longer in Witley, idly speculating as to the probable date of our sailing, whether we were going on the *Olympic* or *Lapland*, or where we would embark, Southampton or Liverpool. The Brigade Orderly Room was haunted by seekers after the truth until in desperation *they* posted a notice on the door, "No, we don't know when we're sailing!" And someone pencilled under it "What do you know?" Then one night before the end of March, the Brigade was mustered over by the road in the darkness; and we were sorted out by Dispersal Areas. When "Baldy" Lewis yelled at the top of his voice like a Grand Trunk brakeman, "Toronto!" or "Montreal!" you felt you were already home and as each contingent lined up they gave the laugh to the districts which were not so well represented in the brigade. A final roll-call by the aid of flashlights and we were off.

About four or five o'clock the following afternoon we tumbled out of the train at Liverpool when the good ladies, whom one always found in any station in the Old Country, were waiting with hot coffee, buns and smokes. It seemed an eternity waiting to go on board - what if something should turn-up to balk us even at that stage? What if the sailors should decide just then to go on strike or somebody start another war somewhere? Oh, tut-tut, let's go! At length we lined up in alphabetical or some sort of disorder and a lusty band played us on board. Clutching our embarkation tickets for dear life lest at the last moment we might miss out we filed up the gangway. It was a great moment and what was that the band was roaring? Oh yes — "The Bells are Ringing (let 'em ring!) for Me and My Gal!"

Now possibly S.S. Northland was not one of these floating palaces or ocean greyhounds but she looked mighty good to us. We'd have been satisfied to travel steerage in a tug and, provided she kept the water out and did her ten miles an hour, that was good enough for us. So we went down below - way down -and located our bunks. There were 118 in our stateroom. "Weary" Beatty and "Kibby" swallowed the rest of the pound bottle of Mothersill's Anti-Seasickness Remedy and lay them down prepared for the worst. It was a little choppy the following morning and it was noticed that some noisy youths, formerly the life of the party, were singularly silent with pre-occupied looks as though expecting a summons. But after the first day we experienced ideal weather and even those who had resigned themselves to a fortnight of *mal du mer* came on deck and took a languid interest in the proceedings.

There is nothing to justify dwelling upon the nature of our passage - every moment the old tub was getting nearer Halifax - that was all that mattered. Then at last we could make out the Canadian shore though we were very close before we could owing to a fog. It would sound foolish now to speak of the funny feeling upon seeing "God's Country" again but in three years it had come to mean a great deal to us. The old signs even had a homely significance to us - such as "Red Rose Tea is Good Tea" - and look at those girls on the pier - no, they're not waving at you, you poor fish! Finally they permitted us to leave the boat and whom should we meet but old Rhude who had beat us home! Yes, it was Rhude but not as we knew him. Smartly attired in form-fitting clothes which we inwardly vowed to duplicate with our first gratuity cheque - he bore no resemblance to the sweet tenor of Don Sub. Yet not so long ago we had seen him in the humble role of day picquet, wielding a dirty broom and exclaiming "Mules shun! From the right tell off in fours!"

According to the district in which we had elected to be demobilized, we were assigned to various trains and, amid the general scattering for coffee and telegram forms, we close this history. In saying "So long" to the fellows themselves, we shall refrain from the usual platitudes, but we hasten to assure any who perchance, misled by these trivial pages, might consider the 43rd men rather a queer outfit, that they were "a fine body of men and done their best for their country."

Now the rest of the acts of the 43rd Battery, and all that they did, are they not written in the book of the Canadian War Records?

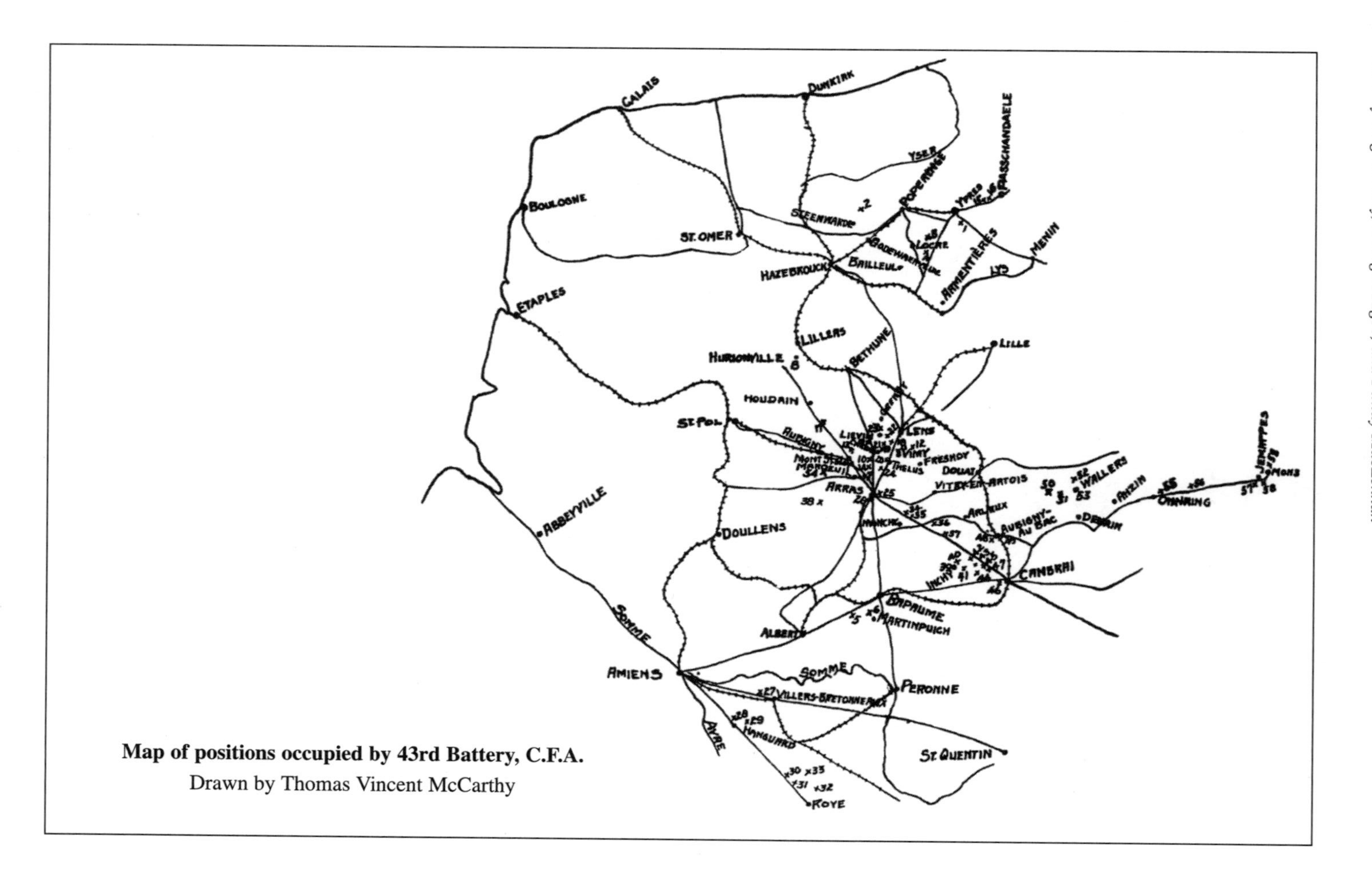

Map of positions occupied by 43rd Battery, C.F.A.
Drawn by Thomas Vincent McCarthy

Appendix One

Battery Positions, 1916-1919

1. Railway Dugouts (Ypres), July 20, 1916 - August 25,1916.
2. Watou (Rest), August 26, 1916 - September 7, 1916.
3. Kemmel, September 9, 1916 - September 16, 1916.
4. Kemmel Hill, September 24, 1916 - October 2, 1916.
5. Somme (Sausage Valley), October 9, 1916 - October 26, 1916.
6. Somme (Martinpuich),October 26, 1916 - November 25, 1916.
7. Maroeuil, November 28, 1916 - February 14, 1917.
8. Hurionville (Rest), February 14, 1917 - March 7, 1917.
9. Carency, March 7, 1917 - March 24, 1917.
10. La Targette (Plank Road), March 24, 1917 - April 16, 1917.
11. Vimy Village, April 16, 1917 - July 11, 1917.
12. Vimy ("Y" Position),July 11, 1917 - September 8, 1917.
13. Le Pendu (Rest), September 10, 1917 - October 10, 1917.
14. Fort George (Rest), October 10, 1917 - October 25, 1917.
15. Passchendaele (Kansas Cross), November 1 - November 27, 1917.
16. Passchendaele (Abraham Heights), Nov. 27,1917 - Dec. 12,1917.
17. Ohlain (Rest), December 15, 1917 - January 17, 1918.
18. Petit Bois (Brick Piles, 2 guns), January 18, 1918 - February 25, 1918.
19. Fosse 6, February 2, 1918 - March 29, 1918.
20. Thelus Caves, March 29, 1918 - April 12, 1918.
21. Angres (4 guns), April 12, 1918 - May 13,1918.
22. Liévin (2 guns), April 12, 1918 - May 13, 1918.
23. Calonne, May 13, 1918 - July 14, 1918.
24. Neuville St. Vaast, July 14, 1918 - July 18, 1918.
25. Arras (Factory), July 19, 1918 - July 21, 1918.
26. Arras (Station), July 21, 1918 - July 29, 1918.
27. Amiens (Bois Abbé), August 3, 1918 - August 6,1918.
28. Hangard, August 6, 1918 - August 9, 1918.
29. Demuin, August 9, 1918.
30. Le Quesnel, August 9, 1918 - August 11, 1918.
31. Folies, August 11, 1918 - August 14, 1918.
32. Fouquescourt, August 14,1918 - August 16,1918.
33. Vrely, August 16,1918 - August 24,1918.
34. Monchy (4 guns), August 28, 1918 - September 1, 1918.

35. Vis-en-Artois (2 guns), August 28, 1918 - September 1, 1918.
36. Boiry, September 1, 1918 - September 2, 1918.
37. Cambrai Road, September 2, 1918 - September 4, 1918.
38. Simencourt (Rest), September 4, 1918 - September 22,1918.
39. Inchy, September 25, 1918 - September 27, 1918.
40. Canal-du-Nord, September 27, 1918.
41. Bourlon Wood (Rear) Sept. 27, 1918.
42. Bourlon Village (Left), September 27 - 28,1918.
43. Bourlon Wood (Left),September 28 - 29,1918.
44. Railway Cutting (Front of Wood),September 29, 1918.
45. Raillencourt Valley, September 29 - 30, 1918.
46. St. Olle, September 30, 1918 - October 2, 1918.
47. Raillencourt Valley, October 2, 1918 - Oct. 9, 1918.
48. Epinoy, October 11, 1918 - October 18, 1918.
49. Aubigny-au-Bac ,October 18, 1918 - October 19, 1918.
50. Somain, October 19, 1918 - Oct. 20, 1918.
51. Helesmes, October 20, 1918 - October 21, 1918.
52. Bois-de-Raismes, October 21, 1918 - October 22, 1918.
53. Wallers (Rest), October 22, 1918 - November 5, 1918.
54. Habarcq (Right Section), Oct. 31, 1918 - November 8, 1918.
55. Onnaing (Front of Village), November 5 - 8, 1918.
56. Quievrain, November 8 - 9, 1918.
57. Jemappes, November 9 - 10, 1918.
58. Jemappes, (Front of Village), November 10 - 11, 1918.
59. Nimy, November 11, 1918 - December 11, 1918.
60. Grez-Doiceau, December 15, 1918 - February 15, 1919.

"Lest We Forget"

Gnr. K.B. DOWNIE, killed August 10, 1916, Ypres.
(Buried in Railway Dugouts Cemetery, Belgium)
Major W. A. IRVING, killed October 11, 1916, Somme.
(Buried in Albert Communal Cemetery, France)
Gnr. P. VAN AUDENARDE, died of wounds, November 14,1916, Somme.
(Buried St. Sever Cemetery, Rouen, France)
Sgt. R.D. TURNBULL, killed April 9,1917, Vimy Ridge.
(Buried Villers Station Cemetery, France)
Dvr. H. McGILLIVRAY, died of wounds, April 21, 1917, Vimy Ridge.
(Buried Aubigny Communal Cemetery, France)
Gnr. G.H. CURZON, died of wounds, May 13,1917, Vimy Village.
(Buried Villers Station Cemetery, France)
Gnr. W. VANT, killed June 5, 1917, Vimy Village.
(Buried Ecoivres Military Cemetery, France)
Lieut. E.P. BLACK, died of wounds, June 8, 1917, Vimy Village.
(Buried Ecoivres Military Cemetery, France)
Bmdr. M. KINNIE, killed June 24. 1917, Vimy Village.
(Buried Ecoivres Military Cemetery, France)
Ftr. O. KNETCHEL killed June 24, 1917, Vimy Village.
(Buried Ecoivres Military Cemetery, France)
Bmbr. F. McCAREY, killed July 7, 1917, "Y" Position, Vimy.
(Buried Ecoivres Military Cemetery, France)
Gnr. J. MOSS, died of wounds, July 7,1917, "Y" Position, Vimy.
(Buried Ecoivres Military Cemetery, France)
Bmbr. S. SCHREITER, died of wounds, August 11, 1917, "Y" Position. Vimy. (Buried Maroeuil British Cemetery, France)
Gnr. A.M. DUNBAR, died of wounds, November 2,1917, Passchendaele.
(Buried Nine Elms British Cemetery, Belgium)
Gnr. H.R. KAY, killed November 6,1917, Passchendaele.
(No known grave; commemorated on thc Menin Gate Memorial)
Gnr. A. BAXENDALL, killed November 8, 1917, Passchendaele.
(Buried Brandhoek New Military Cemetery, No.3, Belgium)
Gnr. C. GIFFORD, killed November 8,1917, Passchendaele.
(Buried Brandhoek New Military Cemeterty, No.3, Belgium)
Gnr. W.A.L. DOWNING, died of wounds, Nov. 8, 1917, Passchendaele.
(Buried Vlamertinghe New Military Cemetery, Belgium)

Bmdr. J.J. GREENLEE, killed November 23, 1917, Passchendaele.
(Buried Brandhoek New Military Cemetery, No.3, Belgium)
Gnr. C. DONAGHY, killed November 25, 1917, Passchendaele.
(Buried Brandhoek New Military Cemetery, No.3, Belgium)
Gnr. A. O'BRIEN, killed November 28, 1917, Passchendaele.
(Buried Oxford Road Cemetery, Belgium)
Gnr. J. MASON, killed December 11, 1917, Passchendaele.
(Buried Brandhoek New Military Cemetery, No.3, Belgium)
Dvr. J. McGILL, died of wounds, April 9, 1918, Mont St.Eloi.
Gnr. C.B. STEVENS, killed May 10, 1918, Liévin.
(Buried Sucrerie Cemetery, France)
Gnr. R. RICE, died of wounds, June 3, 1918, Calonne.
(Buried Fosse No.10 Cemetery, France)
Bmdr. J.D. DOHERTY, died of wounds, July 26,1918, Arras Station.
(Buried Wanquetin Communal Cemetery Extension, France)
Gnr. A. VIENOTTE, died of wounds, September 1, 1918, Monchy.
(Buried Vis-en-Artois British Cemetery, France)
Gnr. W.G. MAGEE, died of wounds, September 27,1918, Bourlon Wood.
(Buried Bucquoy Road British Cemetery, France)
Gnr. J.C. TOZER, died of wounds, October 1, 1918, St. Olle.
(Buried Duisans British Cemetery, France)
Gnr. E. ANGEL, died of wounds, October 16, 1918, Sauchy L'Estrée.
(Buried St. Sever Cemetery, Rouen, France)
Lieut. G.A. COCKBURN, died November 8, 1917, as a Prisoner of War,
(While serving with the Royal Flying Corps.
(Buried Passchendaele New British Cemetery, Belgium)
Dvr. E. KINNIE, died in England, March 20,1918.
(Buried Brookwood Military Cemetery, England)
Gnr. H.G. MASSON, died in Canada, July 3, 1918.
(Buried Prospect Cemetery, Toronto, Canada)
Dvr. A. E. MOTT, died in Canada, March 28, 1919.
(Buried Hamilton Cemetery, Canada)

Appendix Three

43RD BATTERY, CANADIAN FIELD ARTILLERY NOMINAL ROLL

This Nominal Roll of the members, of the 43rd Battery who left Canada or who afterwards joined it, has been compiled from memory only, by James Kingsburgh and others, as all official lists and records were deposited in London prior to the return of the Battery to Canada. Certain omissions are inevitable.

Dvr. Ainsworth, F.
Bmdr. Alford, A.L.
Cpl. Algie, J.
Gnr. Allen, P.
Cpl. Allies, Doc
Bmdr. Anderson. D.E.
Gnr. Anderson, J.C.
Gnr. Angel, E.
Dvr. Archibald, E.B.
Maj. Armitage, R.S.
Gnr. Ashton, W.
Dvr. Ashton, G.G.
Dvr. Austin. R.
Q.M.S. Ball, G.B.
Bmdr. Ballantyne, L.R.
Dvr. Barnes, A.
Sgt. Barnett, J.R.
Pte. Bateman, A.S.
Gnr. Baxendall, A.
Bmdr. Beatty, F.W.
Dvr. Beaumont, B.B.
Dvr. Bell, John
Dvr. Bell, R.W.
Gnr. Belyea, L.J.
Dvr. Bennett, A.
Sgt. Biggs, L.S.
Gnr. Bingham, E.E.
Lt. Black, E.P.
Dvr. Blakely
Gnr. Bodner, C.L.
Lt. Booth, F.H.
Gnr. Booton, W.H.
Cpl. Brackett, A.
Dvr. Bradden, G.R.
Gnr. Brennan, P.J.
Bmdr. Brimson, R.M.
Dvr. Britton, W.D.
Gnr. Brodie, C.M.
Gnr. Brookes, H.F.
Dvr. Brown, Andrew
Dvr. Brown, Archie
Dvr. Brough, W.D.
Dvr. Bruce, W.
Q.M.S. Bubbs, A.
Dvr. Burns, A.G.
Dvr. Burns, Walter
B.S.M. Buss, N.B.
Dvr. Campbell, D.
Gnr. Carmichael, K.K.
Gnr. Carpovitch, F.
Dvr. Carter, J.
Dvr. Carrigan, W.H.
Bmdr. Case, B.S.
Dvr. Cass, H.
Sgt. Caulfield, J.
Sgt. Chace, H.H.
Gnr. Chalk, J.B.
Gnr. Chappelle
Gnr. Chishohn, J.
Lt. Cockburn, G.A.
Sgt. Cockwell, P.D.
Maj. Coghlan, F.T.
Dvr. Comfort
Gnr. Conroy, J.N.
Dvr. Cook, A.
Gnr. Cook, C.C.
Bmdr. Cooke, G.E.
Gnr. Copeland, R.S.
Cpl. Corbett, R.R.
Gnr. Cottle, L.R.
Cpl. Coutts, W.
Bmdr. Cowan, H.
Lt. Cox, A.C.
Maj. Craig, C.S.
Capt. Craig, R.H.
Gnr. Cross, E.
Gnr. Crothers, W.
Lt. Crowe, C.D.
Gnr. Crowley, L.E.
Cpl. Cunningham, F.
Dvr. Culham, G.J.

Gnr. Curzon, G.H.
Q.M.S. Curzon, C.W.P.
Dvr. Davidson, J.
Gnr. Davidge, J.
Gnr. Depper
Dvr. Derby, J.
Dvr. Deruchie, A.J.
Dyr. Diamond, C.S.
Dvr. Dixey, A.
Tptr. Dobson, H.
Bmdr. Doherty, J.D.
Gnr. Donaghy, C.
Capt. Donald, A.S.
Lt. Donnolly, J.T.
Gnr. Douglas
Dvr. Dove, R.C.
Gnr. Downie, K.B.
Gnr. Downing, W.A.L
Gnr. Dunbar, A.M.
Gnr. Edgecombe, J.F.
Gnr. Edwards, W.
Gnr. Elliott
Gnr. Elwell, F.
Gnr. Eneix, B.
Gnr. Etheridge, E.R.
Ftr. Everett, M.F.
Tptr. Fairweather, F.G.
Gnr. Fallis, M.M.
Gnr. Farrell, J.C.
Dvr. Faucett, B.
Dvr. Finch, E.
Gnr. Finnerty, J.
Gnr. Finney, W.J.
Gnr. Fisher, T.
Bmdr. Flesh, C.
Maj. Fletcher
Dvr. Fletcher, W.C.
Dvr. Flint, G.L.
Dvr. Foster, J.
Whlr. Foster
Gnr Fowke, W.
Whlr. Fox, J.
Dvr. Foyston, B.E.
Gnr. Freeman, E.S.
Dvr. Fulford, E.
Dvr. Funnow, G.
Dvr. Galloway, H.
Gnr. Gay, W.
Gnr. Gifford, C.
Dvr. Gleason, M.E.
Capt. Gordon. S.H.
Lt. Gordon, S.
Gnr. Gorman, W.G.
Gnr. Gourley, G.
Lt. Graham, C.C.P.
Gnr. Gratto, H.E.
Gnr. Gray
Sdlr. Gray, Alex
Bmdr. Greenlee, J.J.
Lt. Grier, C.G.M.
Dvr. Grindrod, J.H.
Dvr. Gunning, C.C.
F.Sgt. Harvey, G.
Gnr. Hammond
Dvr. Hayes, F.M.
Dvr. Hill, Grant
Gnr. Hill, T.G.
Cpl. Hill Hugh
Dvr. Hill, Thomas
Dvr. Hobbs, A.G.
Gnr. Hobbs, A.E.
Gnr. Homeyer, H.W.
Dvr. Horn, R.
Dvr. Hornby, A.
Dvr. Horsman, C.
Gnr. Howard, E.F.
Dvr. Howse, W.
Gnr. Hubbell, W.C.
Gnr. Hughes, H.R.
Gnr. Hunt J.D.
Sgt. Irvine, D.R.
Maj. Irving, W.A.
Gnr. Jarman, J.V.
Dvr. Jenkins, T.L.
Gnr. Johnson, F.
Sgt. Junkin, C.I.
Gnr. Kay, H.R.
Gnr. Keates, G.A.
Gnr. Kelley, C.W.
Bmdr. Kelly, R.C.
Dvr. Kemp, F.W.
Lt. Kennedy, H.B.
Gnr. Kerr, C.W.
Dvr. Kilbourne, M.
Gnr. Kimber, W.
F.Sgt. King, J.
Green
Gnr. Kingsburgh, J.
Dvr. Kinnie, C.F.
Dvr. Kinnie, Floyd
Bmdr. Kinnie, M.
Ftr. Knechtel, O.
Gnr. Knight, N.A.
Gnr. Knowles, A.L.
Gnr. Knox, W.H.
Gnr. Knox, John
Sgt. Laird, R.S.
Gnr. Lander, B.C.
Gnr. Lane, A.
Bmdr. Lautenslayer, E.
Lt. Lawrence, C.A.
Dvr. Lee, C.
Gnr. Letheren, C.C.
Gnr. Letheren, Fred
Dvr. Leveille
Dvr. Levette, W.
Cpl. Lillow, A.V.
Gnr. Livingstone, J.H.
Dvr. Lucas, C.P.
Gnr. Lucas, F.E.
Dvr. Lucas, H.J.
Bmdr. Ludgate, H.J.
Dvr. Locke

Gnr. McAdam, A.
Dvr. McAinsh
Bmdr. McArthur, C.E.
Bmdr. McArthur, D.A.
Bmdr. McCarey, F.
Dvr. McCarvell, W.A.
Gnr. McCarthy, T.V.
Lt.-Col. McCrae, D.A.
Lt. McCrudden, H.E.
Dvr. MacDonald, A.
Sgt. McDonald, C.W.
Dvr. McDougall, D.
Gnr. McFaul, J.N.
Dvr. McGhee, D.
Dvr. McGill, J.
Dvr. McGillivray, H.
Gnr. McKay, D.C.
Sgt. McKay, R.A.
Dvr. McKen, James
Gnr. McKen, John
Dvr. McKenzie, J.E.
Cpl. McKenzie, J.R.
Gnr. McKenzie, S.S.
Dvr. McLean, J.
Gnr. McLellan
Gnr. McLennan, F.A.
Dvr. McLeod, J.
Sgt. MacMillan, L.
Dvr. McMullen, G.
Cpl. McMurrer, F.L.
Gnr. McMurrer, W.
Gnr. MacNamara, W.
Cpl. McNaughton, W.
Gnr. McPhail, W.C.
Gnr. McQuarrie, W.C.
Bmdr. Madden, E.
Gnr. Maddocks, W.
Gnr. Magee, W.G.
Dvr. Marshall, N.
Gnr. Mason, J.
Dvr. Mason, Walter R.
Gnr. Masson, H.G.
Gnr. Matthews
Lt. Matthews, H.
Gnr. Maywood
Dvr. Medcraft, G.
Lt. Meldrum, W.D.
Dvr. Midghall, H.J.
Dvr. Moran, P.
Bmdr. Morden, J.R.
Gnr. Moreton
Gnr. Morrison, A.J.
Gnr. Morton, A.F.
Dvr. Morton.
Gnr. Moss, J.
Dvr. Mott, A.E.
Dvr. Mullen, L.W.
Gnr. Mullins, F.
Gnr. Multhop, A.
Gnr. Munn, R.M.
Sgt. Mutchmor, J.R.
Dvr. Murphy, S.
Dvr. Neal, J.
Gnr. Neelands, R.E.K.
Dvr. Nesbitt, O.
Gnr. O'Brien, A.
Gnr. O'Connor, J.T.
Capt. O'Halloran.
Gnr. O'Halloran, C.
Gnr. Olds, H.H.
S.M. Oliver, H.B.
Cpl. O'Neill, T.M.
Gnr. O'Reilly, G.F.
Dvr. Osmond, G.G.
Dvr. Page, E.A.
Gnr. Pangman, R.P.
Gnr. Panter, G.C.
Gnr. Patton, W.J.
Gnr. Peart, S.E.
Dvr. Pegman, E.
Tptr. Perkins, S.G.
Bmdr. Percival, J.T.
Gnr. Perry, C.N.F.
Cpl. Pettitt, J.E.
Dvr. Piergintili, T.
Lt. Pilgrim, E.W.
Gnr. Plunkett, S.
Dvr. Pollard, H.
Dvr. Porteous, J.
Dvr. Potton, E. .
Dvr. Preston, P.F.
Gnr. Price, C.M.
Bmdr. Price, J.S.
Gnr. Pulling, E.W.
Gnr. Purvis, R.E.
Cpl. Rance, J.
Sgt. Reade, R.
Gnr. Reid, G.S.
Gnr. Revell
Gnr. Rhude, S.B.
Gnr. Rice, R.
Bmdr. Richardson, C.P.
Dvr. Ritchie
Gnr. Roberts, N.R.
Dvr. Robertson, R.
Gnr. Robertson, W.L.
Gnr. Robinson
Gnr. Ross, H.S.
Sdlr. Ross, Walter
Dvr. Ruddy, P.
Dvr. Rundle, G.C.
Dvr. Rushton, H.W.
Dvr. Rushton, P.
Gnr. Rushton, Stanley
Gnr. Rutherford, G.H.
Gnr. Ryan, J.J.
Gnr. Sage, H.
Dvr. Salerne, V.H.
Dvr. Saltman, F.E.
Gnr. Sanders, A.F.
Gnr. Sanders, J.H.
Gnr. Saunders, O.
Dvr. Savage, W.J.D.

Lt. Scarth, H.C.
Bmdr. Schreiter, S.
Cpl. Sentner, W.
Gnr. Sephton, P.
Gnr. Seymour, S.
Bmdr. Sharpe, George E.
Bmdr. Sharpe, W.C.
Gnr. Shields
Dvr. Shipman, A.
Sgt. Shank, A.C.
Sgt. Sills, C.P.
Sgt. Simmons, R.S.
Gnr. Simonds, L.
Gnr. Simpson, E.J.
Gnr. Skeen, A.
Cpl. Skinner, R.
Gnr. Skinner, S.G.
Dvr. Slaughter, A.E.
Sdler. Smith, Charles
Dvr. Smith, Fred.
Sgt. Smith, G.L.
Dvr. Smith, O.C.
Gnr. Smyth, C.B.
Dvr. Smythe, G.K.
S.S. Snyder, A.B.
Bmdr. Souster, A.H.
Dvr. Spinks, E.J.
Cpl. Stephens, C.L.
Dvr. Stewart, J.A.
Dvr. Stewart
Gnr. Stevens, C.B.
Gnr. Stone, A.D.
Gnr. Street, W.C.
Dvr. Stolworthy, E.
Cpl. Stout, R.
Cpl. Sullivan
Dvr. Sullivan, J.D.
Gnr. Sullivan, A.
Gnr. Swain, W.
Cpl. Teasdale, C.
Whlr. Tetley, S.H.D.
Dvr. Thomas
Gnr. Thomas, C.G.
Capt. Thomson, E.S.
Dvr. Thomson, E.W.
Capt. Thompson
Dvr. Thompson, J.
Dvr. Tich, L.
Gnr. Toner, E.
Gnr. Tonkin, W.C.
Gnr. Tozer, J.C.
Dvr. Tuckett, J.
Bmdr. Turnbull, N.M.
Sgt. Turnbull, R.D.
Gnr. Van Audenarde, P.
Sgt. Vandrick, J.
Gnr. Vant, W.
Gnr. Vienotte, A.
Dvr. Walker, W.
Dvr. Walsh, J.
Dvr. Ward, D.N.
Gnr. Warrener, H.P.
Gnr. Wartman, C.C.
Dvr. Watham
Lt. Weldon
Gnr. Whalen, E.J.
Dvr. Wheatley, C.
Lt. Whitaker, E.G.
Lt. Williams, S.E.
Tptr. Williams
Gnr. Willman, F.
Sgt. Wilson, George
Sgt. Wilson, Gordon S.
Dvr. Wilson, H.T.
Bmdr. Wilson, John H.
Gnr. Wilson, J.
Dvr. Widdowson, T.
Dvr. Wims
Bmdr. Wolfe, J.B.
Dvr. Wood, S.E.
Gnr. Wood
Gnr. Worth, W.H.
Lt. Wright, G.L.
Bmdr. Wright, R.L.
Gnr. Wrong, H.A.
Gnr. Yates, A.
Lt. Youell, L.L.